MIGHTY
MILITARY
MACHINES

MECHANICAL MUSCLE BEHIND TODAY'S ARMIES

MIGHTY
MILITARY
MACHINES

MECHANICAL MUSCLE BEHIND TODAY'S ARMIES

Jason Turner

MBI Publishing Company

This edition first published in 2002 by MBI Publishing Company, Galtier Plaza, Suite 200
380 Jackson Street, St. Paul, MN 55101-3885 USA

MBI Publishing Company books are also available at discounts in bulk quantity for industrial or sales-promotional use. For details write to Special Sales Manager at Motorbooks International Wholesalers & Distributors, Galtier Plaza, Suite 200, 380 Jackson Street, St. Paul, MN 55101-3885 USA

Library of Congress Cataloging-in-Publication Data Available.
ISBN 0-7603-1409-8

Printed in Hong Kong

Editor: Peter Darman
Picture Research: Andrew Webb
Design: Richard Berry
Production: Matt Weyland

CONTENTS

40.10 WM

The Iveco range of light vehicles was designed for high mobility both on and off road, which makes them ideal for military use. As such, they fill the gap between traditional jeeps and medium trucks. Like many modern utility vehicles, they have been designed for the easy and simple installation of different body types. The heart of the 40.10 is a high-power diesel engine, either a turbo-charged model developing 103 horsepower or a turbo-charged aftercooled version developing 122 horsepower. Use on rough terrain is made easier by the front independent suspension, while the large tyres allow the vehicle to operate in mud, sand or snow. The large radiator cools the engine even in tropical temperatures, while a large and efficient air cleaner ensures suitable filtration in desert conditions. When operating in cold climates, the ambulance can be fitted with a supplementary heater to pre-heat the engine before starting at low temperatures. The body of the cab consists of a steel shell, on the sides of which are fitted fastened panels in glass-reinforced resin. The cab itself can be covered by a tarpaulin or a hard top, and the windscreen can be tilted forward to reduce height to facilitate loading the truck on an aircraft or for parachute drops. A normal ambulance payload is four stretchers.

SPECIFICATIONS

Type:	ambulance
Manufacturer:	Iveco
Powerplant:	Fiat 8142 diesel
Horsepower:	103
Transmission:	5 + 5
Length:	5.5m (18.04ft)
Width:	2m (6.56ft)
Height:	2.86m (9.38ft)
Weight:	4500kg (9900lb)
Ground clearance:	0.4m (1.31ft)
Armament:	none
Crew:	2
Top speed:	100km/h (62.5mph)
Range:	600km (375 miles)
Fording:	0.5m (1.64ft)
Gradient:	60 percent
Configuration:	4 x 4

LAND ROVER

The Land Rover Battlefield Ambulance, based on the TUM chassis, replaced the British Army's fleet of wheeled battlefield ambulances between 1997 and 1999. It has a capacity for a combination of up to four stretcher cases or six seated casualties and provides a very high standard of medical facilities. It is airportable and meets amphibious requirements, making it suitable for rapid deployment to anywhere in the world. There have been three generations of British Army Land Rover ambulances. The First Generation utilized an extended and raised body on either a Series II/IIA or, less commonly, Series III 109in chassis. These were in production from the late 1950s right up to the early 1980s. The Second Generation was based on a rebuilt 101 Forward Control model and had a comparatively short production run. All 101-based ambulances were built between 1981 and 1982 using factory re-manufactured 1976 vehicles, 101FC production having ceased in 1978. The current version, the Third Generation, is based on the military-specified Defender XD130 (and, in this guise, is also known as "Pulse" or, less accurately, "Wolf"). Like all Land Rovers, this model is rugged and can be serviced in the field if need be, and the tools required for this servicing are often just a hammer and a few spanners.

SPECIFICATIONS

Type:	ambulance
Manufacturer:	Land Rover
Powerplant:	300 TDI diesel
Horsepower:	85
Transmission:	5 + 1
Length:	3.72m (12.2ft)
Width:	1.79m (5.87ft)
Height:	1.99m (6.52ft)
Weight:	3700kg (8140lb)
Ground clearance:	0.21m (0.68ft)
Armament:	none
Crew:	3
Top speed:	140km/h (87.5mph)
Range:	500km (312 miles)
Fording:	0.5m (1.64ft)
Gradient:	70 percent
Configuration:	4 x 4

FV 432

First introduced in 1962, the FV series of armoured vehicles was developed to fulfil no less than 14 roles including command post armoured personnel carrier, ambulance, minelayer, recovery and repair vehicle, mortar carrier, radar or troop carrier. Totally nuclear, biological, chemical (NBC) proof, it can carry up to 10 men and 2 crew and may be armed with a 7.62mm machine gun or turret-mounted L37 machine gun. This ubiquitous vehicle fulfils a number of roles for the British Army, including armoured command post, 81mm mortar carrier, artillery observation post, field artillery computer equipment carrier, minelayer, Cymbeline radar carrier, basic troop carrier and ambulance. Each brigade in the British Army has a field ambulance unit that operates in direct support of battle groups. The field ambulance units provide dressing stations where casualties are treated prior to transfer to a field hospital. Vehicles such as the FV 432 provide the field ambulance units with integral ambulance support on the battlefield, which also includes wheeled vehicles. The care of the sick and wounded is the responsibility of the Royal Army Medical Corps, whose personnel in peacetime are based at the various medical installations throughout the world or in field force units.

SPECIFICATIONS

Type:	*ambulance*
Manufacturer:	*GNK Sankey*
Powerplant:	*Rolls-Royce K60 diesel*
Horsepower:	*240hp*
Transmission:	*6 + 1*
Length:	*5.25m (17.22ft)*
Width:	*2.8m (9.18ft)*
Height:	*2.28m (7.48ft)*
Weight:	*15,280kg (33,616lb)*
Ground clearance:	*0.5m (1.64ft)*
Armament:	*none*
Crew:	*2*
Top speed:	*52km/h (32.5mph)*
Range:	*580km (362 miles)*
Fording:	*1m (3.28ft)*
Gradient:	*60 percent*
Configuration:	*tracked*

M997

The M996, M996A1, M997, M997A1, M1035 and M1035A1 High Mobility Multipurpose Wheeled Vehicles (HMMWVs) are the ambulance configuration of the HMMWV family. The vehicles are equipped with basic armour and used to transport casualties from the battlefield to the medical aid stations. The HMMWV's mission is to provide a light tactical vehicle for command and control, special purpose shelter carriers, and special purpose weapons platforms throughout all areas of the modern battlefield. It is supported using the current logistics and maintenance structure established for army wheeled vehicles. The M996/M996A1 are designated as mini-ambulances and can transport up to two litter patients, six ambulatory patients or a combination of litter and ambulatory patients. The M997/M997A1 are designated as maxi-ambulances and can transport up to four litter patients, eight ambulatory patients or a combination of litter and ambulatory patients. The M1035/M1035A1 are soft-top ambulances and can transport up to two litter patients. The vehicles can climb 60 percent slopes and traverse a side slope of up to 40 percent fully loaded. These configurations of the HMMWV are not equipped with the self-recovery winch.

SPECIFICATIONS

Type:	ambulance
Manufacturer:	AM General
Powerplant:	General Motors diesel
Horsepower:	150hp
Transmission:	3 + 1
Length:	5.13m (16.83ft)
Width:	2.15m (7.08ft)
Height:	2.59m (8.5ft)
Weight:	4136kg (9100lb)
Ground clearance:	0.4m (1.31ft)
Armament:	none
Crew:	2
Top speed:	88km/h (55mph)
Range:	539km (337 miles)
Fording:	0.76m (2.5ft)
Gradient:	60 percent
Configuration:	4 x 4

SAMARITAN

The Samaritan is one of the Scorpion family of reconnaissance vehicles, equipped to fulfil the fire support role with a 76mm gun, but also capable of fulfiling to a large degree the anti-tank and reconnaissance roles. The greatly increased mobility afforded by tracks, combined with advanced production techniques, permitted the design of a light, powerful, tracked reconnaissance weapon system with a fire power hitherto unattainable at the weight desired. Costs throughout have been kept down to the minimum, consistent with attaining the objects of mobility, firepower and protection. This has been done by using common components and layout and by using only assemblies and techniques known to be proven. At the same time the most modern materials and methods have been employed. The emphasis throughout has been on simplicity, simplicity in ease of maintenance and in crew training. Similarly inherent reliability has been built in. However, the basic vehicles are capable of sophisticated tasks according to the user's requirements by adding optional equipment such as night-fighting aids, radar and gas detector systems. The Samaritan can accommodate up to six stretchers in the rear compartment, and can be fitted into the fuselage of a C-130 Hercules transport aircraft.

SPECIFICATIONS

Type:	ambulance
Manufacturer:	Alvis
Powerplant:	Jaguar 4.2 litre
Horsepower:	190
Transmission:	7 + 7
Length:	5.07m (16.63ft)
Width:	2.24m (7.34ft)
Height:	2.42m (7.93ft)
Weight:	8660kg (19,052lb)
Ground clearance:	0.35m (1.14ft)
Armament:	none
Crew:	2
Top speed:	72.5km/h (45.31mph)
Range:	483km (302 miles)
Fording:	1.06m (3.47ft)
Gradient:	60 percent
Configuration:	tracked

AVLB

The Armoured Vehicle Launcher Bridge (AVLB) launches a single Close Support Bridge to cross gaps of up to 24.5m (80.38ft) or a combination of such bridges to cross gaps of up to 60m (196.85ft). A single bridge can be laid in about three minutes without exposing the crew to enemy fire. Once the bridge has been laid, the launch vehicle can drive over it and recover it from the far bank. The hull of the AVLB is similar to that of the Chieftain main battle tank, with the driver seated at the front of the hull and the commander and radio operator being behind the driver. The suspension consists of three bogies per side, each bogie having two sets of road wheels and a set of three horizontal springs. The first and last road wheel stations have a hydraulic shock absorber. The bridge girders and launching structure are made of high-strength nickel-alloy steel to facilitate the bearing of armoured fighting vehicles. The bridge is made of two tracks, and each track is capable of bearing the load of light armoured vehicles, thus allowing two-way traffic with vehicles of this size. Each Chieftain bridgelayer usually has one No 8 and one No 9 tank bridge, one carried on the vehicle and the other on a specially adapted Scammel prime mover towing a semi-trailer. The production total for the British Army was 37.

SPECIFICATIONS

Type:	*bridging vehicle*
Manufacturer:	*Vickers Defence Systems*
Powerplant:	*L60 multifuel*
Horsepower:	*730*
Transmission:	*6 + 2*
Length:	*13.74m (45.07ft)*
Width:	*4.16m (13.64ft)*
Height:	*3.92m (12.86ft)*
Weight:	*53,300kg (117,260lb)*
Ground clearance:	*0.5m (1.64ft)*
Armament:	*2 x 7.62mm*
Crew:	*3*
Top speed:	*42km/h (26.25mph)*
Range:	*400km (250 miles)*
Fording:	*1.06m (3.47ft)*
Gradient:	*60 percent*
Configuration:	*tracked*

AVLB

The 26m- (85.3ft-) long MLC 70 LEGUAN Armoured Vehicle Launcher Bridge (AVLB) produced in Germany can be launched from a number of tank chassis, including the following: the American M1A1/A2 "Wolverine" Heavy Assault Bridge (HAB), the German Leopard 1 and the American M60. The bridge itself has been designed for the modern battlefield and possesses the following qualities: bridge laying in less than five minutes, fully automatic launching through an electronically controlled bridge laying system, one-man operation from within the vehicle and with hatch closed, the remote control of a bridge-laying operation via cable connection (when visibility is obstructed at the constructing site), and bridge laying/retrieval in darkness. The bridge can even be modified to act as a ferry for the crossing of very wide waterways. The bridge is placed by the bridgelaying vehicle or tank on pontoons for this application. Hydraulically adjusted ramps are added at the ends of the bridge to make it easier to drive on and off the ferry. The aluminium pontoons feature an integrated pump-jet drive which makes them highly manoeuvrable, permitting movements in shallow water. Continuous crossing of vehicles and equipment is enabled by coupling the individual ferries together so that they form a floating bridge.

SPECIFICATIONS

Type:	bridging system
Manufacturer:	MAN Technologie AG
Powerplant:	MB 873 Ka-501 multifuel
Horsepower:	830
Transmission:	4 + 2
Length:	13.37m (43.86ft)
Width:	4m (13.12ft)
Height:	3.85m (12.63ft)
Weight:	50,000kg (110,000lb)
Ground clearance:	0.42m (1.37ft)
Armament:	none
Crew:	2
Top speed:	62km/h (38.75mph)
Range:	450km (281 miles)
Fording:	1.2m (3.93ft)
Gradient:	60 percent
Configuration:	tracked

BIBER

The Leopard 1-based Armoured Bridgelayer Biber, with a crew of two men, is equipped with a hydraulic bridge system which is laid horizontally (the so-called cantilever principle). This means that it can be used without the disadvantage of being observed some distance away by the enemy. It is operated by the driver via the central hydraulic system and can be laid under armour protection within approximately three minutes, even in the range of enemy small arms. The laying procedure is divided into several stages that are controlled by a sequence control system. The picking up of the bridge can be done either by its own vehicle or another Biber from either side of the defile, by proceeding in reverse sequence. Offering an effective support length of 20m (65.61ft), the Biber bridge consists of two 11m (36.08ft) bridge sections, mounted in two pairs, one above the other on both sides on top of the vehicle in transport mode. The hull of the Biber is almost identical to that of the Leopard 1 main battle tank, with the driver seated at the front of the hull on the right side and the commander in the centre (the engine and transmission are mounted at the rear). The torsion bar suspension consists of seven road wheels with the drive sprocket at the rear and the idler at the front.

SPECIFICATIONS

Type:	*bridging system*
Manufacturer:	*Rheinmetall*
Powerplant:	*MB 873 Ka-501 multifuel*
Horsepower:	*830*
Transmission:	*4 + 2*
Length:	*11.79m (38.68ft)*
Width:	*4m (13.12ft)*
Height:	*3.55m (11.64ft)*
Weight:	*45,300kg (99,660lb)*
Ground clearance:	*0.42m (1.37ft)*
Armament:	*none*
Crew:	*2*
Top speed:	*62km/h (38.75mph)*
Range:	*450km (281 miles)*
Fording:	*1.2m (3.93ft)*
Gradient:	*60 percent*
Configuration:	*tracked*

M3 AMPHIBIOUS RIG

The M3 amphibious bridging and ferry system currently in service with the British Army is a replacement for the earlier M2 system. Improvements include the ability to be driven on land and water from the same end. The four-man crew sit in the cab in the front of the vehicle. Before entering the water, the hydraulically operated hinged buoyancy tanks (which are on top of the vehicle when travelling) are swung through 180 degrees into position. The decking is positioned in a few minutes by a light alloy crane which when travelling is on the centreline of the vehicle. When assembled the roadway is 7.62m (25ft) long and 5.48m (18ft) wide. Once in the water, the units are fastened together to form a Class 50 bridge or ferry. Once in the water the M3 is fully amphibious, with one of the engines driving propellers for sideways movement and the other engine driving a steering propeller. One of the two side propellers can also be used for steering. When the M3 is swimming, the wheels are raised to reduce drag. On land all-wheel steering is possible, and there are flotation bags inside the wheel arches for extra flotation. The M2 and M3 systems were specifically developed for operations with the British Army of the Rhine for the crossing of the many waterways in central Europe.

SPECIFICATIONS

Type:	amphibious bridge
Manufacturer:	EKG
Powerplant:	2 x Deutz Model F8 diesels
Horsepower:	178
Transmission:	unknown
Length:	12.73m (41.76ft)
Width:	3.35m (10.99ft)
Height:	3.93m (12.89ft)
Weight:	25,300kg (55,660lb)
Ground clearance:	0.7m (2.29ft)
Armament:	none
Crew:	4
Top speed:	76km/h (47.5mph)
Range:	725km (453 miles)
Fording:	amphibious
Gradient:	60 percent
Configuration:	4 x 4

M60

The chassis of the M60 armoured vehicle launched bridge (AVLB) is almost identical to that of the M60 main battle tank, though the turret has been removed and the driver sits farther back. The vehicle has torsion bar-type suspension which is made up of six road wheels with the idler at the rear, with three track return rollers. The second and sixth road wheel stations have hydraulic shock absorbers. The bridge itself weighs 13,380kg (29,436lb) and is made of aluminium. On the vehicle it is carried folded and launched over the front hydraulically. When the vehicle has reached the space to be bridged, the bridge is raised hydraulically into the vertical, unfolded and then lowered into place; the launcher is then detached. In general the procedure takes three minutes, with recovery time being between 10 and 60 minutes depending on terrain conditions. The bridge itself has a length of 19.2m (63ft) and can span a gap up to 18.28m (60ft). In the M60 chassis the engine and transmission are at the rear, and the two-man crew consists of a driver and commander. The earlier M48 AVLB had two Browning 12.7mm machine guns, but the M60 variant has no armament. The M60 bridge layer is now being replaced by more modern and capable systems, such as the Wolverine (see page 16).

SPECIFICATIONS

Type:	mechanized bridge
Manufacturer:	General Dynamics
Powerplant:	Continental AVDS-1790-2A
Horsepower:	750
Transmission:	2 + 1
Length:	11.28m (37ft)
Width:	4m (13.12ft)
Height:	3.9m (12.79ft)
Weight:	55,205kg (121,451lb)
Ground clearance:	0.36m (1.18ft)
Armament:	none
Crew:	2
Top speed:	48.28km/h (30.17mph)
Range:	500km (312 miles)
Fording:	1.21m (3.96ft)
Gradient:	30 percent
Configuration:	tracked

WOLVERINE

The Wolverine is an armoured vehicle designed to carry, emplace and retrieve an assault bridge capable of supporting loads such as the M1A2 main battle tank. The Wolverine is a combat support system which integrates advanced bridging, hydraulic and electronic control capabilities into a single survivable system. Wolverine fills the need for a combat gap crossing capability with the same mobility, survivability and transportability as the M1 Abrams tank. Wolverine will be a one-for-one replacement for the Armoured Vehicle Launched Bridge (AVLB) in select heavy divisional engineer battalions, armoured cavalry regiments and heavy separate brigades. Wolverine consists of an M1 Abrams tank chassis modified to transport, launch and retrieve a Military Load Class (MLC) 70 bridge across gaps up to 24m (78.74ft) wide. It is airportable in the C-5A aircraft and is comparable in mobility and survivability to the Abrams tank. A crew of two will operate the system. The bridge, made of four interchangeable sections, is 26m (85.3ft) long, 4m (13.12ft) wide and weighs 10,886 kg (23,949lb). The system launches through automatic suspension and has redundant launch capability using the vehicle powerpack or slaved from another Wolverine. In an emergency the launch sequence can be accomplished by one man.

SPECIFICATIONS

Type:	bridging equipment
Manufacturer:	General Dynamics
Powerplant:	AGT-1500 Turbine
Horsepower:	1500
Transmission:	4 + 2
Length:	13.4m (43.96ft)
Width:	3.48m (11.41ft)
Height:	3.96m (12.99ft)
Weight:	69,800kg (153,560lb)
Ground clearance:	0.48m (1.58ft)
Armament:	none
Crew:	2
Top speed:	72km/h (45mph)
Range:	416km (260 miles)
Fording:	1.21m (4ft)
Gradient:	60 percent
Configuration:	tracked

AAVC7A1

The AAVP7A1 is an armoured assault fully tracked amphibious landing vehicle. The vehicle carries troops in water operations from ship to shore, through rough water and surf zones. It also carries troops to inland objectives after ashore. The primary responsibility of the vehicles during an amphibious operation is to spearhead a beach assault. They disembark from ship and come ashore, carrying infantry and supplies to the area to provide a forced entry into the amphibious assault area for the surface assault element. Once the armoured assault vehicles (AAVs) have landed, they can take on several different tasks: manning check points, Military Operations in Urban Terrain missions, escorting food convoys or mechanized patrol. The AAVC7A1 gives a commander a mobile task force communication centre in water operations from ship to shore and to inland objectives after ashore. The system consists of five radio operator stations: three staff stations, and two master stations. The command communications system contains equipment to provided external secure radio transmission between each AAVC7A1 vehicle and other vehicles and radios. Internal communication between each crew station is provided. The first prototype was built in 1979 and the vehicle entered service in 1983.

SPECIFICATIONS

Type:	*amphibious command vehicle*
Manufacturer:	*FMC Corporation*
Powerplant:	*Cummins Model VT400*
Horsepower:	*400*
Transmission:	*6*
Length:	*7.94m (26.04ft)*
Width:	*3.27m (10.72ft)*
Height:	*3.26m (10.69ft)*
Weight:	*23,072kg (50,758lb)*
Ground clearance:	*0.4m (1.31ft)*
Armament:	*1 x 7.62mm*
Crew:	*3*
Top speed:	*72km/h (45mph) (land)*
Range:	*480km (300 miles)*
Fording:	*amphibious*
Gradient:	*60 percent*
Configuration:	*tracked*

FOX

The Fox is a rolling laboratory that takes air, water, and ground samples and immediately analyzes them for signs of weapons of mass destruction. The Fox M93A1 Nuclear, Biological and Chemical Reconnaissance System (NBCRS) is intended to improve the survivability and mobility of US Army ground forces by providing increased situational awareness and information superiority to head-quarters and combat manoeuvre elements. NBC defence encompasses three major functions: contamination avoid-ance, protection and decontamination. Contamination avoid-ance is the concept of avoiding contamination whenever pos-sible and is the focal point of NBC defence doctrine. With the ability to provide rapid, accurate chemical and radiologi-cal contamination information to these elements, the NBCRS vehicle forms a key portion of the full-dimensional protection concept. The onboard M21 Remote Sensing Chemical Agent Alarm allows the crew to detect chemical agent clouds as far as 5m (3.12 miles) away. The crew can perform chemical and radiological reconnaissance operations while operating in a shirt-sleeve environment inside the NBCRS vehicle, even while the vehicle is operating in a con-taminated area. The Fox saw valuable service with Coalition forces during the 1991 Gulf War.

SPECIFICATIONS

Type:	*mobile laboratory*
Manufacturer:	*General Dynamics*
Powerplant:	*Mercedes-Benz Model OM*
Horsepower:	*320*
Transmission:	*7 + 1*
Length:	*6.3m (20.66ft)*
Width:	*2.98m (9.77ft)*
Height:	*2.3m (7.54ft)*
Weight:	*17,000kg (37,400lb)*
Ground clearance:	*0.5m (1.64m)*
Armament:	*none*
Crew:	*3*
Top speed:	*105km/h (65.62mph)*
Range:	*800km (500 miles)*
Fording:	*amphibious*
Gradient:	*70 percent*
Configuration:	*6 x 6*

LAV-C2

The Light Armoured Vehicle-Command and Control (LAV-C2) is an all-terrain, all-weather vehicle with night capabilities. It allows a commander the capability to command, control and communicate (C3) the activities of his forces under full armoured protection. This mobile command station provides field commanders with all necessary resources to control and coordinate light armoured units in all assigned roles. It is air transportable via C-130, C-141, C-5 and CH-53 E aircraft. When combat loaded there are 200 ready rounds and 800 stowed rounds of 7.62mm ammunition. The vehicle can be made fully amphibious within three minutes. Another variant of the LAV is the LAV-C2 Fire Direction Centre (FDC), whose mission is to control and assign fire missions, choose the number and the type of rounds to fire, and provide firing data to eight mortars under platoon operations or four under split section operations. It maintains continuous communications via digital or voice with all platoon elements within its area of responsibility, forward observers, fire support elements and higher headquarters. The FDC performs fire planning and target prioritizing and coordinates with other fire support assets, combat support and combat service support, as needed.

SPECIFICATIONS

Type:	command and control
Manufacturer:	General Motors
Powerplant:	Detroit Diesel 6V53T
Horsepower:	350
Transmission:	5 + 1
Length:	6.42m (21.08ft)
Width:	2.48m (8.16ft)
Height:	2.79m (9.16ft)
Weight:	12,818kg (28,200lb)
Ground clearance:	0.57m (1.87ft)
Armament:	1 x 7.62mm
Crew:	5
Top speed:	100km/h (62mph)
Range:	656km (410 miles)
Fording:	amphibious (with preparation)
Gradient:	60 percent
Configuration:	8 x 8

MEWSS

The Mobile Electronic Warfare Support System (MEWSS) is the US Marine Corps' ground component of the Intelligence and Electronic Warfare Common Sensor (IEWCS) system. It uses the same subsystems as the US Army's Ground Based Common Sensor-Light and Heavy (GBCS-L &GBCS-H), and the Advanced Quickfix (AQF). The MEWSS uses the Light Armored Vehicle (LAV) as its platform. Its mission is as follows: two-way communications, data collection, locating and positioning of enemy forces, jamming and intercepting enemy communications, and the mobile support of friendly units The MEWSS is capable of intercept and location. It is also capable of conducting surgical electronic attacks against designated targets and is operated in the forward area of operations. The most notable example of IEWCS technology transfer is to the US Marine Corps in an electronics suite upgrade to the Mobile Electronic Warfare Support System (MEWSS), known as the MEWSS Product Improvement Program (MEWSS-PIP). This upgrade utilizes all three IEWCS subsystems configured in a standard Light Armored Vehicle, to become in essence a fourth IEWCS platform configuration. The vehicle can be made fully amphibious, and has a swim speed of 9.6km/h (6mph).

SPECIFICATIONS

Type:	electronic warfare
Manufacturer:	General Motors
Powerplant:	Detroit Diesel 6V53T
Horsepower:	350hp
Transmission:	5 + 1
Length:	6.57m (21.58ft)
Width:	2.49m (8.2ft)
Height:	2.64m (8.66ft)
Weight:	12,818kg (28,200lb)
Ground clearance:	0.5m (1.64ft)
Armament:	1 x 7.62mm
Crew:	5
Top speed:	100km/h (62mph)
Range:	410km (250 miles)
Fording:	amphibious (with preparation)
Gradient:	60 percent
Configuration:	8 x 8

PIRANHA ACV

The Mowag Piranha III family of vehicles offers the features and performances required of a modern, multi-role vehicle, which is well suited to practically any battlefield or peace-keeping/peace-enforcing role anywhere in the world, either as an armoured personnel carrier or an ideal platform for a complete range of weapons systems from small-calibre turrets up to the high firepower of a 105mm gun. The Armoured Command Vehicle (ACV) is in Swedish Navy service, being deployed to the coastal artillery brigades. It is a highly mobile, well protected command, control, communications and information platform whose crew members are protected from light machine-gun rounds and artillery shell splinters by hardened steel plate armour. The crew compartment is fully air conditioned, while the vehicle has been designed to operate in a nuclear, biological and chemical (NBC) environment. The vehicle is highly mobile: a hydropneumatic system with a MOWAG-designed height adjustment system at all wheel stations in combination with the new wheels system with CTIS and ABS and the choice of tyre sizes to suit any type of terrain, as well as high power-to-weight ratio power packs, have resulted in a class of wheeled vehicles with a mobility comparable to tracked vehicles, whilst still retaining air transportability.

SPECIFICATIONS

Type:	command and control
Manufacturer:	Mowag
Powerplant:	Scania DSJ9-48A
Horsepower:	387
Transmission:	7 + 1
Length:	7.91m (25.95ft)
Width: .	2.6m (8.53ft)
Height:	2.91m (9.54ft)
Weight:	20,000kg (44,000lb)
Ground clearance:	0.45m (1.47ft)
Armament:	1 x 7.62mm
Crew:	up to 8
Top speed:	100km/h (62.5mph)
Range:	500km (312 miles)
Fording:	1.5m (4.92ft)
Gradient:	60 percent
Configuration:	10 x 10

PIRANHA ASV

The Piranha armoured sensor vehicle (ASV) is in service with the Swedish Navy. It is a highly mobile sensor vehicle for the direction of artillery fire and the detection of both land and air targets. The spacious command room in the rear of the vehicle houses four consoles. The vehicle can be deployed very quickly and can operate in hostile environments. One reason for this is the Piranha'a excellent payload-versus-combat weight qualities. The new Piranha III design provides the customer with flexibility in the choice of protection levels and equipment/weapons integration and personnel transport. Through the modular concept, the question is how much payload/volume is required and not the number of axles/wheels, because the front section of the vehicle, including the two front steered axles, is identical on the 6 x 6, 8 x 8 and 10 x 10 versions of the Piranha III vehicles. The use of the Piranha family vehicles by peace-keeping forces has proven the inherent protection of the vehicle design, especially against mines. The knowledge gained through the experiences of the peace-keeping missions, for example in former Yugoslavia and Somalia, has been implemented in the variable protection concept, which allows ballistic protection to be tailored to meet the expected threat in each mission scenario.

SPECIFICATIONS

Type:	*fire direction vehicle*
Manufacturer:	*Mowag*
Powerplant:	*Scania DSJ9-48A*
Horsepower:	*400hp*
Transmission:	*7 + 1*
Length:	*9.6m (31.49ft)*
Width:	*2.6m (8.33ft)*
Height:	*3.82m (12.53ft)*
Weight:	*23,000kg (50,600lb)*
Ground clearance:	*0.45m (1.47ft)*
Armament:	*1 x 7.62mm*
Crew:	*6*
Top speed:	*100km/h (62mph)*
Range:	*450km (281 miles)*
Fording:	*1.5m (4.92ft)*
Gradient:	*60 percent*
Configuration:	*10 x 10*

XA-202

This is the XA-202 Command Version of the XA-200 series. It features a hydraulic mast and communications gear. The vehicle is well armoured and heavily modified, the heavy machine-gun mount has been moved from the crew compartment hatch to the vehicle commander's hatch. The telescopic mast is powered by the main engine hydraulic pump and has hydraulic support legs for the vehicle and an automatic guy rope system of 5.2m (17.06ft) radius with hydraulic tightening system. The mast takes two people about 10 minutes to deploy. The hull is divided into four sections: operator room, driver/commander compartment, engine room and auxiliary power unit (APU) room. The 10 kW diesel APU is installed for the operator room equipment. Add-on armour provides protection from up to 12.7mm armour-piercing shells. There are four fitting points for VHF antennas. The add-on armour plates can be added by the crew thanks to their relatively small size and with maximum armour the amphibious capabilities are only partially lost. The vehicle can still, however, drive through 1.5m (4.92ft) of water. If a client demands both heavy armour and amphibious capability, the vehicle can be modified to solve this problem without compromising the armour protection or the amphibious characteristics.

SPECIFICATIONS

Type:	*command vehicle*
Manufacturer:	*Patria*
Powerplant:	*Valmet 612 turbocharged diesel*
Horsepower:	*270*
Transmission:	*6 + 1*
Length:	*7.41m (24.31ft)*
Width:	*2.92m (9.58ft)*
Height:	*2.92m (9.58ft)*
Weight:	*23,000kg (50,600lb)*
Ground clearance:	*0.45m (1.47ft)*
Armament:	*1 x 12.7mm machine gun*
Crew:	*2 + 4*
Top speed:	*90km/h (56.25mph)*
Range:	*600km (375 miles)*
Fording:	*1.2m (3.93ft)*
Gradient:	*60 percent*
Configuration:	*6 x 6*

ATLAS

The ATLAS is the next generation military, variable reach, rough terrain forklift vehicle selected by the Department of the Army. It is capable of lifting 4545kg (10,000lb). The front end quick attach feature can accommodate dual carriages of 2727kg (6000lb) and 4545kg (10,000lb) each. The intended use of the ATLAS includes selecting stock from storage; stuffing and unstuffing containers; and unloading, transporting, and loading boxes. It is capable of mobility in rough terrain and is transportable in C-130 aircraft. The ATLAS System Description is a four-wheel drive, pneumatic tired, diesel engine-driven, variable reach, boom type forklift truck with a maximum speed of 23mph. The rated capacity of the ATLAS is 2727kg (6000lb) at 0.6m (2ft) load centre (with a 2727kg [6000lb] capacity carriage mounted) and 10000lb at 1.21m (4ft) load centre (with the 4545kg [10,000lb] capacity carriage mounted). TRAK International manufactured the 6000M variable reach forklifts between 1989 and 1993 and delivered over 2200 vehicles to the US armed forces. These logistic support vehicles performed exceedingly well during Operation Desert Storm in 1991 and in Bosnia handling missiles, ammunition, and supplies in the toughest types of terrain in direct support of deployed military forces.

SPECIFICATIONS

Type:	forklift
Manufacturer:	TRAK
Powerplant:	Cummins 4BT3 diesel
Horsepower:	116
Transmission:	4 + 3
Length:	4.3m (14.1ft)
Width:	2.5m (8.2ft)
Height:	3m (9.84ft)
Weight:	11,951kg (26,323lb)
Ground clearance:	0.44m (1.44ft)
Armament:	none
Crew:	1
Top speed:	32km/h (20mph)
Range:	400km (250 miles)
Fording:	unknown
Gradient:	60 percent
Configuration:	4 x 4

BM 440

The BM 440 has been specifically designed to handle North Atlantic Treaty Organization (NATO) pallets. In addition, other design features have been included for military use. With the breakup of the Warsaw Pact and the USSR, the emphasis for Western European and American forces has switched from a confrontation in central Europe to peace-keeping in Europe and military operations outside the European theatre. Armed forces therefore need to be able to move quickly at relatively short notice, and their logistical backup has to be similarly mobile. Therefore, the BM 440 has a low-profile cab for air portability. It also has a high road speed to enable it to keep up with convoys, and can also be towed at convoy speeds. The operator's cab is mounted at the front to provide good visibility with minimum engine noise and vibration. It has a forward reach capability to allow loading and unloading from one side of a cargo truck or rail wagon. Power-operated steering reduces driver discomfort, and the forklift can be fitted with a range of attachments, including buckets and sweepers to increase its versatility. The models shown above are in service with the British Army, and are painted white because they part of a United Nations commitment.

SPECIFICATIONS

Type:	*forklift*
Manufacturer:	*Volvo*
Powerplant:	*TAD420 diesel*
Horsepower:	*140*
Transmission:	*4 + 3*
Length:	*5.62m (18.43ft)*
Width:	*2.54 (8.33ft)*
Height:	*2.67m (8.75ft)*
Weight:	*7000kg (15,400lb)*
Ground clearance:	*0.4m (1.31ft)*
Armament:	*none*
Crew:	*1*
Top speed:	*60km/h (37.5mph)*
Range:	*500km (312 miles)*
Fording:	*0.75m (2.46ft)*
Gradient:	*60 percent*
Configuration:	*4 x 4*

M320.42 WM

Iveco of Italy produces a range of light, medium and heavy military trucks unrivalled by any other manufacturer in the world. Iveco trucks are in active service throughout the world supported by a comprehensive international dealer organization. Their range is very comprehensive: at the light end of the weight range is a 4 x 4 with a payload of 1500kg (3300lb) based on the class-leading Turbo Daily chassis. This highly flexible vehicle can be adapted for use in a wide variety of roles, including troop transporter, command post, light gun tractor and ambulance. Moving to higher-capacity vehicles, a recent addition to the range is the outstanding Multipurpose Military Vehicle – (MMV). This is a high-mobility 4 x 4 offroad truck with a payload capability of up to 6400kg (14,080lb). It is C-130 Hercules transportable and the cab area is easily armoured with the addition of appliqué panels. Available in three engine sizes, three wheel base lengths and with manual or automatic transmissions, the MMV can be tailored to meet a wide variety of military uses. The M320 mobile crane is just one of Iveco's products. With outriggers the crane can lift up to 30,000kg (66,000lb), while without outriggers the load that can be lifted can be up to 8500kg (18,700lb). This means it can lift both trucks and light armoured fighting vehicles.

SPECIFICATIONS

Type:	mobile crane
Manufacturer:	Iveco
Powerplant:	Iveco CURSOR 10 diesel
Horsepower:	420
Transmission:	6 + 6
Length:	10m (32.8ft)
Width:	2.13m (7ft)
Height:	3.03m (9.94ft)
Weight:	12,200kg (26,840lb)
Ground clearance:	0.5m (1.64ft)
Armament:	none
Crew:	1
Top speed:	90km/h (56.25mph)
Range:	500km (312 miles)
Fording:	1m (3.28ft)
Gradient:	60 percent
Configuration:	8 x 8

RTCC

The Grove Manufacturing Corporation produces a number of mobile hydraulic cranes for the military and civilian markets. The Rough Terrain Container Crane (RTCC) has a galvanized steel cab which has an opening skylight with electric wiper, deluxe seat with arm rest-integrated crane controls, hydraulic oil heater plus drive and steering controls. The RTCC is built for heavy work. For example, it has four hydraulically telescoping beams with "inverted" jacks and outrigger pads. Each one has independent horizontal and vertical movement control from the crane operator's cab. The vehicle has a standard Graphic Display load moment and anti-block system with audio-visual warning and control lever lock-out. These systems provide electronic display of boom angle, length, radius, tip height, relative load moment, maximum permissible load, and load indication. The main and auxiliary hoists each have two vane motors, planetary gear and dual speed with automatic spring-applied multi-disc brakes. The company produces five types of hydraulic cranes for the military market: truck-mounted cranes, rough terrain cranes, all-purpose warehouse cranes, all terrain cranes and hydraulic lattice boom cranes. There are nearly 300 RTCCs currently in US Army service.

SPECIFICATIONS

Type:	*rough terrain crane*
Manufacturer:	*Grove Manufacturing Corporation*
Powerplant:	*Cummins 6CTA diesel*
Horsepower:	*250*
Transmission:	*6 + 6*
Length:	*14.34m (47.04ft)*
Width:	*3.34m (10.95ft)*
Height:	*3.97m (13.02ft)*
Weight:	*49,500kg (108,900)*
Ground clearance:	*0.53m (1.73ft)*
Armament:	*none*
Crew:	*1*
Top speed:	*40km/h (25mph)*
Range:	*400km (250 miles)*
Fording:	*unknown*
Gradient:	*76 percent*
Configuration:	*8 x 8*

RTCH

The Army Standard 50K Rough Terrain Container Handler (RTCH) is a modified commercial truck which is essentially a Caterpillar model 988B wheel loader with a CAT model AH60 forklift mast. It is used in conjunction with 6.09m (20ft), 10.66m (35ft) or 12.19m (40ft) top handler attachments for lifting containers weighing up to 25,000kg (55,000lb). In its standard configuration, the RTCH can stack containers two high. It is designed to function over rough terrain and through salt water up to 1.52m (5ft). Its primary use is in holding and marshalling areas by selected supply, ammunition and transportation units. There are two known non-standard variants of the RTCH. The first results from the installation of a fork kit that was issued only to Fort Eustis concurrent with the initial fielding of the RTCH. So equipped, the RTCH can function as a rough terrain forklift. This fork kit is not currently available in the US Army supply system. The second RTCH variant comes from installing a low-mount fork assembly that allows the RTCH to lift half-height – 1.29m (4.25ft) – containers. Sixty-two kits were fielded between April and September 1992. Fort Eustis has about half of all those produced. This half height kit is not available through the US Army supply system.

SPECIFICATIONS

Type:	forklift
Manufacturer:	Caterpillar
Powerplant:	Caterpillar 3408
Horsepower:	393
Transmission:	powershift
Length:	10.73m (35.2ft)
Width:	3.5m (11.48ft)
Height:	4.11m (13.48ft)
Weight:	5000kg (11,000lb)
Ground clearance:	0.4m (1.31ft)
Armament:	none
Crew:	1
Top speed:	40km/h (25mph)
Range:	unknown
Fording:	1.52m (4.98ft)
Gradient:	30 percent
Configuration:	4 x 4

RV730

This vehicle is designed for recovery operations of tracked vehicles. It is based on a 6 x 6 chassis and is built for heavy recovery operations, winching, towing and hoisting. The main recovery winch has a capacity of 20,000kg (44,000lb) single pull and is mounted in the slewing frame of the crane. The mounting of the winch in the slewing crane base means that the object is always being pulled in a direct line towards the recovery vehicle, thus facilitating the lifting of heavy loads. The crane itself is hydraulically operated between horizontal and 70 degrees, and the arm has a hydraulic telescopic extension that works with a full load. The crane can be operated from the seat of the crane base or from a remote-control unit. At the rear of the vehicle is a lifting/towing boom that is hydraulically operated; it has a maximum lifting capacity of 6000kg (13,200lb). Mounted behind the cab are locked cabinets that accommodate tools and accessories necessary for the lifting mission. The outriggers are used as anchoring spades and have been designed so that each one can carry the pulling force of 40,000kg (88,000lb). However, this is possible only when loads are being pulled from the rear. Sideways, the pulling force is limited to 15,000kg (33,000lb).

SPECIFICATIONS

Type:	*recovery vehicle*
Manufacturer:	*Hägglunds Moelv*
Powerplant:	*DS11 diesel*
Horsepower:	*305*
Transmission:	*9 + 1*
Length:	*8.8m (28.87ft)*
Width:	*2.5m (8.2ft)*
Height:	*3.25m (10.66ft)*
Weight:	*21,000kg (46,200lb)*
Ground clearance:	*0.45m (1.47ft)*
Armament:	*none*
Crew:	*1*
Top speed:	*100km/h (62.5mph)*
Range:	*500km (312 miles)*
Fording:	*1.1m (3.6ft)*
Gradient:	*30 percent*
Configuration:	*6 x 6*

AEV

The German Armoured Engineer Vehicle (AEV) is based on the Leopard 1 main battle tank chassis. It has been modified by replacing the turret with a new welded top structure. In addition, the AEV is equipped with a dozer blade, excavator and two winches. The dozer blade has two rippers for tearing up roads and other hard surfaces, and the dozer itself can be tilted, elevated and skewed thanks to a unique hydraulic design. The main use of the blade is for digging, though the blade can also be used as a soil anchor when operating the winches or the excavator. The AEV has a hinged excavator arm mounted on a turntable at the centre front of the vehicle. The excavator has a digging sector of around 175 percent at the front of the vehicle with operation similar to commercial excavators. There is also a grabbing claw for lifting timber logs which is fitted to the underside of the excavator arm. The two hydraulic capstan winches are designed for the recovery of other vehicles plus self-recovery. They provide great flexibility and have a pulling power of up to 60,000kg (132,000lb). The two-man crew are under armour protection in the vehicle at all times, allowing for excavating to be carried out under enemy fire. The AEV is a valuable asset in the German Army arsenal.

SPECIFICATIONS

Type:	armoured engineer vehicle
Manufacturer:	Hägglunds Moelv
Powerplant:	MTU MB 838 Ca M500
Horsepower:	830
Transmission:	4 + 2
Length:	10m (32.8ft)
Width:	3.6m (11.81ft)
Height:	3m (9.84ft)
Weight:	46,000kg (101,200lb)
Ground clearance:	0.44m (1.44ft)
Armament:	none
Crew:	2
Top speed:	62km/h (38.75mph)
Range:	650km (406 miles)
Fording:	4m (13.12ft)
Gradient:	50 percent
Configuration:	tracked

AVRE

This British Assault Vehicle Royal Engineers (AVRE) consists of a Chieftain main battle tank with the turret and all armament removed and a metal plate fitted that covers the turret ring. The driver's position remains unaltered with a hatch, but the AVRE commander's position has been fitted with a hatch. Over the entire length of the vehicle are two rails, on which up to three maxi-pipe fascines or up to five rolls of Class 60 trackway can be carried. They are unloaded by raising the rails at the rear. At the front of the vehicle is a dozer blade or mine plough and at the rear is a winch. In the centre of the AVRE is a crane with a telescopic jib. This vehicle, of which 50 are in operation with the British Army, is a replacement for the Centurion AVRE that had been in service since the 1960s. The AVRE can also tow the Giant Viper mine-clearing equipment, which consists of a hose filled with plastic explosives that is packed coiled in box mounted on a two-wheel trailer. The hose is fired across a minefield by a cluster of eight rocket motors, and then detonates once it has landed. The crew of the AVRE consists of three men, and no armament is carried other than personal small arms. A dozer blade can also be fitted to the vehicle for the clearing of mines.

SPECIFICATIONS

Type:	armoured engineer vehicle
Manufacturer:	Royal Ordnance
Powerplant:	Roll-Royce CV12
Horsepower:	730
Transmission:	5 + 2
Length:	10m (32.8ft)
Width:	3.92m (12.86ft)
Height:	3m (9.84ft)
Weight:	49,000kg (107,800lb)
Ground clearance:	0.46m (1.5ft)
Armament:	none
Crew:	3
Top speed:	34km/h (21.25mph)
Range:	176km (110 miles)
Fording:	1.45m (4.75ft)
Gradient:	60 percent
Configuration:	tracked

BADGER

The Badger armoured engineer vehicle is based on the Leopard 1 main battle tank, and was developed to meet the special needs of the German Army and combines well-proven components with advanced technology. Its features include extendible dozer blade, scarifiers and cutting and welding equipment, powerful telescopic excavator and an electrically controlled hydraulic system. Like other members of the Leopard family, the Badger has a deep fording capacity of 4m (13.12ft), and even when operating underwater many operational functions are still possible. For example, the vehicle can be underwater in a river while its excavator can be working on one of the river banks. Reflecting the changing role of many of Western Europe's armed forces, Badger has proved a reliable vehicle for defence and peace-keeping missions, as well as for disaster relief operations. They have been successfully deployed in various UN and peace-keeping operations. Its main missions are as follows: preparing river crossings, preparing and removing obstacles and blockades on the battlefield, recovery assistance for deep-fording and underwater main battle tanks, loading loose materials and debris on to trucks, lifting loads during pioneer missions, and the general recovery of vehicles and equipment both on and off the battlefield.

SPECIFICATIONS

Type:	armoured engineer vehicle
Manufacturer:	Rheinmetall
Powerplant:	MTU MB 838 Ca M500
Horsepower:	830
Transmission:	4 + 2
Length:	8.37m (27.46ft)
Width:	3.25m (10.66ft)
Height:	2.57m (8.43ft)
Weight:	43,000kg (94,600lb)
Ground clearance:	0.44m (1.44ft)
Armament:	none
Crew:	3
Top speed:	62km/h (38.75mph)
Range:	650km (406 miles)
Fording:	4m (13.12ft)
Gradient:	50 percent
Configuration:	tracked

BUFFALO

The Buffalo armoured recovery vehicle (ARV) was specifically designed to support the Leopard 2 main battle tank in both the German and Dutch armies and it was developed, produced and delivered to them by Rheinmetall Landsysteme as general contractor. By using the Leopard 2 chassis and proven and modified Leopard 2 assemblies, combined with a powerful recovery system, Rheinmetall Landsysteme has created a recovery vehicle which is superior in its class and meets all mission-related requirements. The Buffalo is equipped with a 35,000kg (77,000lb) capstan winch, a 30,000kg (66,000lb) crane system, an integrated test system and a support and dozer system. Future Buffalos will have a new navigation and control system, a performance-improved auxiliary winch and a liner interior protection system, as well as an advanced optical system for reverse cruise. Upon request, a special launch system for various ammunition, including high-explosive ammunition, can be installed. The missions of the vehicle include the recovery of tracked vehicles out of trenches and rivers, towing tracked vehicles, the recovery of main battles tanks, plus general dozing and obstacles removal duties. Spain and Sweden have placed orders for this Leopard 2-based ARV.

SPECIFICATIONS

Type:	armoured recovery vehicle
Manufacturer:	Rheinmetall
Powerplant:	MTU MB 873 Ka-501
Horsepower:	850hp
Transmission:	4 + 2
Length:	9.07m (29.75ft)
Width:	3.54m (11.61ft)
Height:	2.99m (9.8ft)
Weight:	54,300kg (119,460lb)
Ground clearance:	0.51m (1.67ft)
Armament:	none
Crew:	3
Top speed:	68km/h (42.5mph)
Range:	650km (406 miles)
Fording:	4m (13.12ft)
Gradient:	60 percent
Configuration:	tracked

CEBARV

CEBARV, the Centurion Beach Armoured Recovery Vehicle, is the only recovery vehicle in service in the United Kingdom in the amphibious role. It was developed from the Centurion main battle tank with a prefabricated turret to enable it to ford up to depths of 2.9m (9.51ft). The main tasks of the CEBARV are to recover drowned or broken vehicles; to push off beached landing craft using its built-in special nose block; and to provide a breakwater for small craft and men operating in the water. The CEBARV will be replaced by the Future Beach Recovery Vehicle (FBRV) for the UK's Royal Marines, and it has now been delivered to the UK by prime contractor Hägglunds Moelv of Norway. The FBRV is based on a German Krauss-Maffei Wegmann Leopard 1 main battle tank chassis especially modified for the new mission. It will replace the current Centurion Beach Armoured Recovery Vehicle, which was based on a Centurion Mk 3 main battle tank chassis. The FBRV will be used for a wide range of roles including unbeaching, unbroaching and anchoring of landing craft as well as the recovery of drowned vehicles. In addition, it will provide a lee for recovery and diving operations. The beach recovery vehicle is certainly among the most unusual elements in the British arsenal.

SPECIFICATIONS

Type:	beach recovery vehicle
Manufacturer:	Vickers Defence
Powerplant:	Meteor Mk 6
Horsepower:	650
Transmission:	5 + 2
Length:	8.07m (26.47ft)
Width:	3.4m (11.15ft)
Height:	3.45m (11.31ft)
Weight:	40,000kg (88,000lb)
Ground clearance:	0.45m (1.47ft)
Armament:	none
Crew:	4
Top speed:	33.7km/h (21mph)
Range:	400km (250 miles)
Fording:	2.9m (9.51ft)
Gradient:	60 percent
Configuration:	tracked

CET

The Combat Engineer Tractor (CET) provides support for the British Army battle group by carrying out excavating earth, preparation of river banks, road repair, recovering damaged vehicles and preparing or clearing obstacles. The hull is made of aluminium, and inside the hull the driver sits at the front and operates the winch, with the bucket operator to his rear. Both crew members can reverse their seats to carry out each other's duties if need be. The crew compartment itself is provided with two hatch covers and 10 vision blocks, and is fully air conditioned. The engine and transmission are mounted at the right side of the hull with the final drives being mounted at the front of the hull. The CET has torsion bar-type suspension with five road wheels (the fifth one acts as the idler). The tracks are made of cast steel with rubber bushes and rubber pads are supplied to reduce wear when operating on roads. With preparation the CET is fully amphibious, with steering in the water carried out by deflecting the thrust from water jets mounted on either side of the hull. The two-speed winch has a maximum pull of 8000kg (17,600lb) and is provided with 113m (37ft) of cable. The vehicle also has a rocket-launched ground anchor (shown being fired in the above photograph).

SPECIFICATIONS

Type:	armoured engineer vehicle
Manufacturer:	Royal Ordnance
Powerplant:	Rolls-Royce C6TFR diesel
Horsepower:	320
Transmission:	4 + 4
Length:	7.3m (23.95ft)
Width:	2.76m (9.05ft)
Height:	3.41m (11.18ft)
Weight:	17,700kg (38,940lb)
Ground clearance:	0.45m (1.47ft)
Armament:	1 x 7.62mm
Crew:	2
Top speed:	56km/h (35mph)
Range:	320km (200 miles)
Fording:	1.63m (5.34ft)
Gradient:	60 percent
Configuration:	tracked

CRRAV

CRRAV – Challenger Repair and Recovery Armoured Vehicle – is the most powerful armoured recovery vehicle available today. Its winch capacity enables it to undertake over 80 percent of recovery tasks on a 65,000kg (143,000lb) main battle tank with a single line pull. Its crane has a lift capacity of 6500kg (14,300lb) for automotive assembly exchange and it is fitted with a full electric arc welding facility, air compressor with power tools and track cutter. Its hydraulically operated dozer blade acts as an earth anchor during winching operations, enabling it to exert a maximum line pull of 100,000kg (220,000lb), as well as making it capable of moving large volumes of soil and digging tank scrapes. The majority of CRRAV's repair and recovery equipment is hydraulically powered. It makes maximum use of major automotive sub-systems and components common to the Challenger 2 main battle tank, which enhances its ability to remain on station with, and give close support to, Challenger 2-equipped battle groups. CRRAV has been developed with reliability and maintainability as major design factors. A comprehensive logistic support package, covering every aspect of training, spares and engineering support, keeps the vehicle at the peak of operational effectiveness.

SPECIFICATIONS

Type:	repair & recovery vehicle
Manufacturer:	Vickers Defence Systems
Powerplant:	Perkins CV 12 diesel
Horsepower:	1200
Transmission:	6 + 2
Length:	9.59m (31.46ft)
Width:	3.62m (11.87ft)
Height:	3m (9.84ft)
Weight:	62,000kg (136,400lb)
Ground clearance:	0.5m (1.64ft)
Armament:	1 x 7.62mm
Crew:	3 + 2
Top speed:	59km/h (36.87mph)
Range:	500km (312 miles)
Fording:	1.07m (3.51ft)
Gradient:	58 percent
Configuration:	tracked

CS-563

The CS-433C and CS-563D Vibratory Rollers are both built by Caterpillar in the United States. The CS-433C Vibratory Roller is a commercial compactor which has been modified and manufactured for distribution to military engineers for their compaction requirements. Caterpillar vehicles are an integral part of US Army engineer operations. The CS-433C is equipped with military modifications such as lifting eyes/tie-downs to permit military transport. It also contains a rifle bracket, and in its military configuration a top coat of CARC paint is applied. The machine is capable of compacting a 0.3m (1ft) lift at the rate of 734 cubic yards per hour to a level of 95 on the Proctor scale. The CS-563C Vibratory Roller (pictured) is currently being manufactured for the military engineers for their compaction missions. It contains all of the attributes explained above for the CS-433C, but, in addition, it is capable of compacting a 0.3m (1ft) lift at the rate of 1907 cubic yards per hour. Both compactors are air deployable and have C-130 Drive-On/Drive-Off capabilities. The CS-433C can also be deployed by Low Velocity Air Drop (LVAD). Both machines come equipped with a smooth drum and a pad foot shell kit or pad foot drum and a levelling blade.

SPECIFICATIONS

Type:	roller
Manufacturer:	Caterpillar
Powerplant:	Caterpillar 3116T diesel
Horsepower:	153
Transmission:	unknown
Length:	4.57m (15ft)
Width:	2.13m (7ft)
Height:	2.74m (9ft)
Weight:	10,875kg (23,925lb)
Ground clearance:	0.48m (1.57ft)
Armament:	none
Crew:	1
Top speed:	6.4km/h (4mph)
Range:	unknown
Fording:	unknown
Gradient:	60 percent
Configuration:	wheels & roller

DEUCE

Caterpillar has designed and manufactured a new high-speed dozer for the US Army, the Deployable Universal Combat Earthmover, or DEUCE. These machines perform typical engineering missions, such as vehicle/crew fighting positions, force protection for command posts, artillery and logistics, and disaster relief such as floods. The DEUCE features Caterpillar's Mobil-Trac System (MTS) rubber-belted undercarriage for onroad and offroad mobility and flotation. The DEUCE is a 35,500lb (16,140kg) earthmover capable of highway speeds of over 48km/h (30mph). The hydro-pneumatic suspension can be engaged for cross-country traverses or locked out to provide a stable dozing platform. Two modes of operation – self-deployable for high-speed travel, and earthmoving for dozing – are designed to provide optimum performance for mission flexibility. The DEUCE can be prepared for air drops by two mechanics in less than 20 minutes, and can be re-assembled in less than 30 minutes. C-130 Drive-on/Drive-off preparation takes less than 10 minutes to collapse the front suspension cylinders to lower overall height. Maintainability is a built-in feature of the DEUCE, and accessibility to filters, batteries and fluid sight gauges is easily accomplished.

SPECIFICATIONS

Type:	*earthmover*
Manufacturer:	*Caterpillar*
Powerplant:	*Caterpillar Model 3126 diesel*
Horsepower:	*265*
Transmission:	*automatic*
Length:	*6.42m (21.08ft)*
Width:	*2.94m (9.66ft)*
Height:	*2.71m (8.91ft)*
Weight:	*16,136kg (35,000lb)*
Ground clearance:	*0.3m (1ft)*
Armament:	*none*
Crew:	*1*
Top speed:	*52.8km/h (33mph)*
Range:	*320km (200 miles)*
Fording:	*0.91m (3ft)*
Gradient:	*30 percent*
Configuration:	*tracked*

FODEN RECOVERY VEHICLE

This is a heavy recovery vehicle employed primarily in support of the wheeled logistic vehicle fleet to recover immobilized vehicles as a result of bogging, breakdown or damage. Fitted with an hydraulically operated winch/crane in conjunction with outriggers to lift and recover as required. Slewing cranes, which could be used for various lifting tasks in addition to suspended tows during recovery, were deemed important, thus the Foden vehicle featured a pedestal mounted crane. In addition, instead of having hydraulic rams to raise the main recovery supporting boom, it was lifted by the crane. Once at the required height, either for stowage or with a casualty attached, the boom was locked into position, with pins passing through quadrants on each side of the channel in which the boom moved. This removed the weight from the crane itself which in some cases was then necessarily stowed off the centreline in order to clear the raised boom and casualty. Hydraulic systems were retained to operate the side stabilizers used during crane operations, the rear spade anchors and also a rear axle lockout system. Another feature is a remote-control cable system for operating switches. This allows the recovery mechanic to stand next to the casualty and observe closely while controlling lifts or winching.

SPECIFICATIONS

Type:	recovery vehicle
Manufacturer:	Foden
Powerplant:	Perkins Eagle diesel
Horsepower:	290
Transmission:	9-speed constant mesh
Length:	9.06m (29.72ft)
Width:	2.48m (8.13ft)
Height:	3.35m (10.99ft)
Weight:	25,338kg (55,744lb)
Ground clearance:	0.42m (1.37ft)
Armament:	none
Crew:	1
Top speed:	97km/h (60.62mph)
Range:	500km (312 miles)
Fording:	1.22m (4ft)
Gradient:	33 percent
Configuration:	6 x 6

LAV-R

The Light Armoured Vehicle-Recovery (LAV-R) is an all-terrain, all-weather vehicle with night capabilities. This vehicle is capable of safely uprighting overturned LAVs while minimizing additional damage. It has the tactical mobility to reach and recover/support disabled vehicles. The vehicle is capable of towing a disabled LAV with suspension damage. It is air transportable via C-130, C-141, C-5 and CH-53 E aircraft. The vehicle can be made fully amphibious within three minutes. Though a recovery vehicle, it has the means for self-defence, being equipped with a pintle mount for an M240E 7.62mm machine gun, M257 smoke grenade launchers, 200 rounds of 7.62mm ammunition and a further 800 rounds of 7.62mm ammunition stowed. It has the following hatches: overlapping rear doors, rigger's hatch with left and right covers, commander's hatch, driver's hatch, engine compartment hatch and grills, and front stowage compartment hatch. Communications systems include AN/VIC-2C Intercom System, VHF SINCGARS radios, VHF radio AN/PRC-68 (stowed), UHF Position Location Reporting System and antenna. The boom crane has a 256-degree traverse, remote control, overload protection, two outriggers and two stabilizers.

SPECIFICATIONS

Type:	recovery/support
Manufacturer:	General Motors
Powerplant:	Detroit Diesel 6V53T diesel
Horsepower:	275
Transmission:	5 + 1
Length:	7.24m (24.16ft)
Width:	2.77m (9.08ft)
Height:	2.72m (8.92ft)
Weight:	12,857kg (28,320lb)
Ground clearance:	0.5m (1.64ft)
Armament:	1 x 7.62mm
Crew:	3
Top speed:	100 km/h (62mph)
Range:	656km (410 miles)
Fording:	amphibious
Gradient:	60 percent
Configuration:	8 x 8

M9 ACE

The M9 Armoured Combat Earthmover (ACE) is a highly mobile, armoured, amphibious combat earthmover capable of supporting forces in both offensive and defensive operations. It performs critical combat engineer tasks such as digging fighting positions for guns, tanks and other battlefield systems to increase their survivability. The ACE breaches berms, prepares anti-tank ditches, prepares combat roads, removes roadblocks and prepares access routes at water obstacles. The engine, drive train and driver's compartment are laid out in the rear of the vehicle, while the front features a bowl, apron and dozer blade. Armour consists of welded aluminum with selected steel and aramid-laminated plates. An armoured cupola containing eight vision blocks covers the driver's compartment. The vehicle hull is a welded and bolted aluminum structure with a two-speed winch, and towing pintle and airbrake connections are provided. It is equipped with a unique suspension system which allows the front of the vehicle to be raised, lowered or tilted to permit dozing, excavating, rough grading and ditching functions. In addition, the M9 has armour protection against small-arms and artillery fragmentation, a smoke screening capability and chemical and biological protection for the operator.

SPECIFICATIONS

Type:	armoured earthmover
Manufacturer:	HARSCO Corporation
Powerplant:	Cummins V903C
Horsepower:	295
Transmission:	6 + 2
Length:	6.24m (20.5ft)
Width:	3.2m (10.49ft)
Height:	2.66m (8.75ft)
Weight:	25,000kg (55,000lb)
Ground clearance:	0.33m (1.1ft)
Armament:	none
Crew:	1
Top speed:	48km/h (30mph)
Range:	368km (230 miles)
Fording:	0.91m (3ft)
Gradient:	60 percent
Configuration:	tracked

M88A1

Based on the suspension and running gear of the M48A2 tank, the M88 can be used for both medium and heavy recovery operations using an "A'" frame-type hoisting boom. The superstructure and crew compartment is composed of a single large armour casting and provides protection against most types of machine guns and artillery fragments. First accepted into the US Army's inventory in 1959, over 1000 M88s were produced by Bowen-McLaughin-York of Pennsylvania and powered by a Continental AVSI-1790-6A engine with an Allison XT-1400-2 transmission. The crew comprise commander, driver, mechanic and rigger. Both the driver and mechanic are located at the front of the crew compartment with the driver on the left side. The commander is in the centre under the cupola with the rigger directly behind him. Each crew member has a hatch in the roof of the cab, the commander has his cupola and there is also a door in each side of the superstructure. Armament is a 12.7mm machine gun externally mounted on the vehicle commander's cupola. The US Army and US Marines developed a bulldozer blade which could be retrofitted to an M48A3 tank (then designated M8A3). The M88 is still in service with the US Army and with the Israeli Army.

SPECIFICATIONS

Type:	recovery vehicle
Manufacturer:	BMY Combat Systems Division
Powerplant:	12-cylinder diesel
Horsepower:	750
Transmission:	combined transmission
Length:	8.27m (27.13ft)
Width:	3.43m (11.25ft)
Height:	3.13m (10.26ft)
Weight:	50,803kg (111,766lb)
Ground clearance:	0.43m (1.41ft)
Armament:	1 x 12.7mm
Crew:	4
Top speed:	42km/h (26.25mph)
Range:	300 miles (187 miles)
Fording:	1.4m (4.6ft)
Gradient:	60 percent
Configuration:	tracked

M728

The M728 is a fully tracked armoured vehicle which consists of a basic M60A1 tank with a hydraulically operated debris blade, a 165mm turret mounted demolition gun, a retractable boom and a winch. The demolition gun may be elevated or depressed for use at various ranges and is coaxial mounted with a 7.62mm machine gun. A .50-calibre machine gun is cupola mounted. A mine-clearing rake was specially designed and fabricated to be a "tool" for the M728 in Desert Storm. The M728 was placed in service in 1965 with a total of 291 vehicles. Currently, improvements for the vehicle are being implemented, which will ensure that the M728 remains a valuable asset until replacement vehicles are fielded. During Operation Desert Storm in 1991 it proved unable to manoeuvre with the heavy force due to the inability of the M60 chassis and power train to keep pace with the MIA1 tanks. There were also difficulties associated with maintaining an obsolete, low-density piece of equipment. Such was the case with the mine rake mounted on the M728. Many manoeuvre units simply left the M728 behind rather than slow their advance. Commanders planned for their use as a part of a deliberate breaching operation, but left them behind once they began the pursuit and exploitation phase of the operation.

SPECIFICATIONS

Type:	combat engineer vehicle
Manufacturer:	Detroit Tank Arsenal
Powerplant:	Continental AVDS diesel
Horsepower:	750
Transmission:	2 + 1
Length:	8.97m (29.42ft)
Width:	3.71m (12.17ft)
Height:	3.23m (10.59ft)
Weight:	52,200kg (114,840lb)
Ground clearance:	0.45m (1.47ft)
Armament:	1 x 165mm
Crew:	4
Top speed:	50km/h (31.25mph)
Range:	450km (281 miles)
Fording:	1.2m (3.93ft)
Gradient:	60 percent
Configuration:	tracked

SAMSON

When the CVR(T) series of aluminium armoured light vehicles was designed, a full range of variants was considered including an armoured recovery vehicle. The basic hull of the Spartan was adapted to contain a winch which was operated to the rear of the vehicle. A hinged spade anchor was designed in two halves to preserve access to the rear door. To winch any heavy vehicles or lighter ones from difficult slopes, it is necessary to lay out several pulleys to get the maximum effect from a fairly low-capacity winch. The CVR(T) series of vehicles came into use in the early 1970s and most types are still current. Armoured regiments, infantry battalions and similarly sized units with large amounts of equipment have their own Royal Engineers Light Aid Detachment (LAD), commanded by a captain. These units deploy with their parent unit and are equipped with vehicles such as the Samson. An LAD can vary in size from 25 to 90 personnel, depending on the equipment supported. As the name suggests, the LAD specialises in quick repairs at or near the point of failure, using tools and spares carried by the unit. If the requirement for a longer or more complex repair is diagnosed, the LAD will either call forward a team from the supporting battalion or arrange to have the failed equipment towed to the rear.

SPECIFICATIONS

Type:	armoured recovery vehicle
Manufacturer:	Alvis Vehicles
Powerplant:	Jaguar 4.2-litre petrol
Horsepower:	200
Transmission:	6 + 1
Length:	4.79m (15.71ft)
Width:	2.36m (7.74ft)
Height:	2.25m (7.38ft)
Weight:	8730kg (19,206lb)
Ground clearance:	0.35m (1.14ft)
Armament:	1 x 7.62mm
Crew:	3
Top speed:	72.5km/h (46mph)
Range:	750km (468.75 miles)
Fording:	1.06m (3.47ft)
Gradient:	60 percent
Configuration:	tracked

AARDVARK

The Aardvark Mk4 clears anti-tank and anti-personnel landmines by either detonation or disruption, and is capable of operating in the majority of terrain and environmental conditions encountered in minefields throughout the world. The Mk4 is effective in a variety of soil types and mixes on both flat and undulating ground with gradients of up to 30 percent. It will clear dense surface scrub of 3m (9.84ft) in height and trees with a trunk diameter of 150mm (5.9in), and it will also take out booby traps and trip wires. The cab is a fully armoured structure equipped with 56mm (2.2in) armoured glass windows which are additionally protected by an internal polycarbonate liner and steel grill on the outside. There are facilities for one operator and one additional crew. The inner walls of the crew compartment are lined with a soundproof material and the cab temperature conditions are controlled with heater/air conditioner units. The cab floor has an armour-plated double skin with the lower underside having an angled profile, specifically designed to provide maximum deflection of blast forces. The flail rotor rotates at approximately 300 rounds per minute, with six striker tips striking the ground at any one time, and every piece of ground being struck at least twice.

SPECIFICATIONS

Type:	*mine clearer*
Manufacturer:	*Aardvark Clear Mine Ltd*
Powerplant:	*New Holland in-line diesel*
Horsepower:	*160*
Transmission:	*16 + 16*
Length:	*8.4m (27.55ft)*
Width:	*2.53m (8.3ft)*
Height:	*3.19m (10.46ft)*
Weight:	*11,506kg (25,313lb)*
Ground clearance:	*0.38m (1.24ft)*
Armament:	*none*
Crew:	*1*
Top speed:	*20km/h (12.5mph)*
Range:	*unknown*
Fording:	*0.5m (1.64ft)*
Gradient:	*30 percent*
Configuration:	*semi-tracked*

KEILER

The Keiler mine clearer was developed to meet German Army operational requirements regarding the mobility and flexibility of mechanized brigades. The vehicle has been designed to clear a lane of mines 120m (393ft) long, to a depth of 250mm (9.84in) and 4.70m (15.41ft) wide in under 10 minutes. Keiler offers excellent results compared to all other known mine clearing systems, and the crew are under armour protection during all operations. The vehicle can clear both anti-personnel and anti-tank mines in uneven terrain and different soil structures. This is possible because of an onboard sensor control which ensures maximum clearing. Keiler either explodes all mines in front of the vehicle or throws them aside. By means of the cantilever arm, the clearing system is moved from travelling to clearing position, and a tilt and elevation system serves for terrain adjustment. The carrier arm and the clearing shaft frame are driven by hydro-engines. The clearing shaft itself has 24 flails, and is stowed on top of the vehicle while travelling. When ready for operation the clearing shaft is swivelled to the front and locked, with all processes carried out automatically. In total the German Army has ordered 24 Keiler mine clearers, and some have seen service in the former Yugoslavia with UN peacekeeping forces.

SPECIFICATIONS

Type:	mine clearer
Manufacturer:	Rheinmetall
Powerplant:	MTU MB 871 Ka 501
Horsepower:	800
Transmission:	hydro-mechanical
Length:	10.7m (35.1ft)
Width:	6.35m (20.83ft)
Height:	2.76m (9.05ft)
Weight:	53,000kg (116,600lb)
Ground clearance:	0.44m (1.44ft)
Armament:	none
Crew:	2
Top speed:	72km/h (45mph)
Range:	600km (375 miles)
Fording:	1.45m (4.75ft)
Gradient:	60 percent
Configuration:	tracked

M1 MINE CLEARER

The M1 Mine Clearing Blade System is an auxiliary piece of equipment necessary for the tank unit to breach minefields during the normal conduct of operations. In Operation Desert Storm in 1991 track-width mine ploughs proved very successful against pressure-fused anti-tank mines and allowed the M1A1 main battle tank to breach minefields with little loss of momentum. It is electrically operated and is capable of clearing surface or buried mines up to 1.82m (6ft) in front of the tank's path without the aid of supporting forces or additional equipment. In the 1991 Gulf War the M1A1 chassis proved to be fully capable of ploughing, in desert soils, at rates of 30km/h (18.75mph). This chassis, combined with a full-width plough, will provide a full-width breaching capability that will be able to clear all known mines and still be able to manoeuvre with the heavy force. The plough should be fitted with a wire cutter and be capable of ploughing at variable depths, and should be actuated in the centre to allow the blade to be used for digging trails and survivability positions. While this is not its primary mission, it enhances the capabilities of the US Army engineer force. The specifications at right refer to the mine plough only and not the M1 Abrams main battle tank it is attached to.

SPECIFICATIONS

Type:	*mine plough*
Manufacturer:	*Israel Military Industries*
Powerplant:	*n/a*
Horsepower:	*n/a*
Transmission:	*n/a*
Ploughing depth:	*0.3m (0.98ft)*
Ploughed width each side:	*1.15m (3.77ft)*
Lifted height above ground:	*1.6m (5.24ft)*
Chain track in centre:	*0.71m (2.32ft)*
Ground clearance:	*n/a*
Armament:	*n/a*
Crew:	*n/a*
Clearing speed:	*6.5km/h (4.06mph)*
Range:	*n/a*
Fording:	*n/a*
Gradient:	*30 percent*
Configuration:	*n/a*

M60 MINE PLOUGH

The M60's mine plough (identical to that fitted on the M1 Abrams) is electrically operated and is capable of clearing surface or buried mines up to 1.82m (6ft) in front of the tank's path without the aid of supporting forces or additional equipment. The adaptation is accomplished by using an adaptor kit and an electrical power interface kit. While the plough is a useful addition to the tank's capabilities, the M60 mine ploughs were found wanting during the 1991 Gulf War, where they proved unable to manoeuvre with US heavy forces due to the inability of the M60 chassis and power train to keep pace with the MIA1 tanks. Engineers also had difficulties associated with maintaining an obsolete, low-density piece of equipment. Many units simply left this equipment behind rather than slow their advance during combat operations. Commanders planned for their use as a part of the deliberate breaching operation of Iraqi defences, but left them behind once they began the pursuit and exploitation phase of the mission. US commanders were unanimous in their opinion that the engineer force needs M1 chassis for heavy breaching and gap-crossing equipment. The specifications at right refer to the mine plough only and not the M60 tank it is attached to.

SPECIFICATIONS

Type:	*mine plough*
Manufacturer:	*Israel Military Industries*
Powerplant:	*n/a*
Horsepower:	*n/a*
Transmission:	*n/a*
Ploughing depth:	*0.3m (0.98ft)*
Ploughed width each side:	*1.15m (3.77ft)*
Lifted height above ground:	*1.6m (5.24ft)*
Chain track in centre:	*0.71m (2.32ft)*
Ground clearance:	*n/a*
Armament:	*n/a*
Crew:	*n/a*
Clearing speed:	*6.5km/h (4.06mph)*
Range:	*n/a*
Fording:	*n/a*
Gradient:	*30 percent*
Configuration:	*n/a*

MINE CLEARER

This vehicle is based on the German Leopard 1 main battle tank chassis, with the turret removed and a new top structure added by the manufacturer, Hägglunds Moelv of Norway. The vehicle is equipped with a flail-based clearing system, external drive system, lane-marking system and an overhead weapons station. The chassis has been modified with an anti-spall liner and mine protection. The new welded top structure has the same armour protection as the rest of the vehicle. The mine-clearing unit itself is mounted on a turntable at the front of the vehicle. The flail system is hydraulically driven and clears a 4m- (13.12ft-) wide safe lane for following tracked vehicles. In transportation mode, the flail is rotated and stored on the top of the vehicle. In operating mode, an external drive system is activated which allows the vehicle to run at a constant speed. As well as the flails, the vehicle can operate the following equipment: explosive mine clearing equipment, electronic mine clearing and detection equipment and a lane-marking system. The vehicle is capable of clearing both anti-tank and anti-personnel mines, and mines that are both laying on the surface or buried. The forward flails and an armoured body ensure that the two-man crew are fully protected at all times against mine detonation.

SPECIFICATIONS

Type:	mine clearer
Manufacturer:	Hägglunds Moelv AS
Powerplant:	MTU MB 838 Ca M500
Horsepower:	830hp
Transmission:	4 + 2
Length:	9.9m (32.48ft)
Width:	4.8m (15.74ft)
Height:	3m (9.84ft)
Weight:	47,000kg (103,400lb)
Ground clearance:	0.44m (1.44ft)
Armament:	1 x 7.62mm
Crew:	2
Top speed:	65km/h (40.62mph)
Range:	600km (375 miles)
Fording:	4m (13.12ft)
Gradient:	60 percent
Configuration:	tracked

MINE GUZZLER

The Mine Guzzler is based on a double-track arrangement used commercially. A demining roller is carried on hydraulic supports at the front of the vehicle and powered by an engine with hydrostatical drive. The demining roller, which is tiltable to follow ground undulations, is adjustable for depth and has automatic deepholding. It is made up of a series of plates fitted with tungsten carbide teeth which either cause the mines (anti-personnel and anti-tank) to detonate or chew them into small pieces. Damaged plates can easily be replaced by oxyacetylene cutting and welding in the field. Each vehicle has one spare roller to allow the demining work to continue when a roller is under repair. A complete roller change can be effected in less than 30 minutes using the hydraulic supports to lift the roller for access or to load/unload the roller onto a transport vehicle. The Mine Guzzler can clear mines to a depth of 500mm (19.68in) and over a width of 3.2m (10.49ft). Maximum demining speed is 4km/h (2.5mph). The Mine Guzzler may be operated either by remote control, using onboard television cameras, or from the protection of the driver's cabin, which is protected against fragments by a raised armoured superstructure. Mine Guzzler is built to stand detonations from individual explosives up to 12kg (26.4lb) in weight.

SPECIFICATIONS

Type:	demining roller
Manufacturer:	Bofors Defence
Powerplant:	Scania DSI 14 diesel
Horsepower:	860
Transmission:	hydrostatic
Length:	8.56m (28ft)
Width:	4.12m (13.51ft)
Height:	3.58m (11.74ft)
Weight:	47,000kg (103,400lb)
Ground clearance:	0.4m (1.31ft)
Armament:	none
Crew:	1
Top speed:	6.4km/h (4mph)
Range:	160km (100 miles)
Fording:	1m (3.28ft)
Gradient:	30 percent
Configuration:	tracked

RA-140

This vehicle is designed to clear mines in non-combat conditions, such as humanitarian missions. Although the cabin is armoured it is nowhere near sufficient for in-combat mine clearing. The vehicle is fitted with a 82-chain flail that is powerful enough to destroy the mines (both anti-tank and anti-personnel) before they even detonate. The vehicle is blast-protected and is not damaged even by detonating 10kg (22lb) anti-tank mines. Driving backwards, it clears a path over 3m (9.84ft) wide with a maximum speed of 6km/h (3.75mph) (scatterable mines) or 3km/h (1.87mph) (all other types). The chain rotor consists of 82 chains that whip the ground when rotating, thus detonating or breaking all known mines currently in service. The cabin is completely protected against 7.62mm rounds and against possible shrapnel or fragments from detonating mines or mortar and artillery shells. It is also blast-protected and sound isolated. During transportation the rotor is removed and placed on the vehicle. If the vehicle only has to move a short distance, the rotor is simply lifted hydraulically. The wheels are also bulletproof and mine resistant. The vehicle can be armed with a 12.7mm heavy machine gun, and it also has a camouflage system similar to the one on the XA-180 series.

SPECIFICATIONS

Type:	*mine clearer*
Manufacturer:	*Patria*
Powerplant:	*Deutz, turbocharged, air-cooled*
Horsepower:	*187*
Transmission:	*4 + 1*
Length:	*9.5m (31.16ft)*
Width:	*2.90m (9.51ft)*
Height:	*2.86m (9.38ft)*
Weight:	*15,000kg (33,000lb)*
Ground clearance:	*0.4m (1.31ft)*
Armament:	*1 x 12.7mm*
Crew:	*1*
Top speed:	*70km/h (43.75mph)*
Range:	*250km (156 miles)*
Fording:	*0.8m (2.62ft)*
Gradient:	*60 percent*
Configuration:	*4 x 4*

RHINO

In terms of efficiency, safety, and clearing capacity, the mine clearing system RHINO represents a new generation of large-area mine-clearing systems. Based on well-proven construction machine technology, RHINO offers the maximum in reliability, easy maintenance and servicing. The system was especially developed for humanitarian clearing operations, and consists of an unmanned basic vehicle, a specially designed mine-clearing unit and a mobile control station. Due to RHINO's solid construction and its remote control, optimum safety for the vehicle itself and the crew members during the entire clearing operation is ensured. Even after the detonation of anti-tank mines, the vehicle itself remains undamaged. All material is forced through a gap between two counter-rotating drums. Mines either explode or are destroyed mechanically, so that neither anti-personnel nor anti-tank mines remain intact. The drums are equipped with easy-to-change, long-lasting tungsten carbide chisels. RHINO was delivered to Croatia in August 1998 and has successfully proven its efficiency in all clearing operations of the Croatian demining service. Further RHINO systems were deployed in clearing operations in several countries such as Cambodia, Jordan and South Korea for clearing missions on the border with North Korea.

SPECIFICATIONS

Type:	demining roller
Manufacturer:	Rheinmetall
Powerplant:	Caterpillar diesel
Horsepower:	650
Transmission:	unknown
Length:	9.6m (31.49ft)
Width:	3m (9.84ft)
Height:	3.15m (10.33ft)
Weight:	58,000kg (127,600lb)
Ground clearance:	0.4m (1.31ft)
Armament:	none
Crew:	1
Top speed:	3.8km/h (2.3mph)
Range:	unknown
Fording:	1.2m (3.93ft)
Gradient:	30 percent
Configuration:	tracked

CRUSADER

The Scammell Crusader is essentially a standard civilian vehicle modified to fulfil military requirements. Two basic models were produced, both of which are in service with the British Army. The first, known as the 20-ton tractor, has a two-man cab, and the second, the 35-ton tractor, has a three-man cab. The cab is mounted on the chassis by two rubber-brushed trunnion mountings at the front and two coils sprung with integral telescopic dampers at the rear. The engine is the same in the two models, though the one in the 35-ton model is coupled to an RTO 915 manual gearbox with 15 forward and three reverse gears. Mounted to the rear of the cab is a winch that has a maximum capacity of 8000kg (17,600lb) at a speed of 27.2mm (1.07in) per minute. The winch can be used either to the front or rear and is fitted with an overload warning bell. The front suspension comprises longitudinal semi-elliptical springs; the rear suspension comprises fully articulated, inverted longitudinal semi-elliptical springs. The 20-ton model has 9 forward and 1 reverse gears. Steering is power assisted on both models. The specifications at right refer to the 35 t model. The tyres in the pictures have been prepared for use on snow and ice. This vehicle is in British Army use.

SPECIFICATIONS

Type:	*tank transporter*
Manufacturer:	*Scammell*
Powerplant:	*Rolls-Royce 305 Mk III*
Horsepower:	*305*
Transmission:	*15 + 3*
Length:	*6.66m (21.85ft)*
Width:	*2.5m (8.2ft)*
Height:	*3.3m (10.82ft)*
Weight:	*11,095kg (24,409ft)*
Ground clearance:	*0.5m (1.64ft)*
Armament:	*none*
Crew:	*1*
Top speed:	*65km/h (40.62mph)*
Range:	*500km (312 miles)*
Fording:	*0.76m (2.49ft)*
Gradient:	*20 percent*
Configuration:	*6 x 4*

FH16 6 X 6

The emphasis on durability has been a feature of Volvo products ever since the company started operating in 1927. Volvo developed a driven front axle as early as 1937, heralding the birth of Volvo all-wheel drive (AWD). The first Volvo all-wheel drive (AWD) truck was introduced in 1939 in the Swedish Army. Since then Volvo has produced more than 30,000 AWD vehicles, from the smallest in today's range, the workhorse in the three- to five-tonne payload model with a six-litre turbocharged diesel engine, to heavy duty, high technology battle-tank transporters with a 16-litre turbocharged diesel engine. The Volvo FH16 6 x 6 is the Volvo heavy tank transporter with a Volvo D16, 16-litre, in-line electrically controlled diesel engine with an output of 520 horsepower at 1800rpm, and equipped with a Volvo EPG engine brake of 374 brake horsepower at 2200rpm. The customer has a choice of the Volvo Powertronic gearbox or an automatic five- or six-speed transmission. In order to utilize the best performance and achieve maximum driveability, the Powertronic can also be equipped with an integrated primary retarder. This gives very high braking power, not only at high speed. Easy tank loading/unloading is done by using two 20-tonne winches that can be manoeuvred separately and at different speeds.

SPECIFICATIONS

Type:	tank transporter
Manufacturer:	Volvo
Powerplant:	D16 16-litre diesel
Horsepower:	520
Transmission:	16 + 1
Length:	7.56m (24.8ft)
Width:	2.5m (8.2ft)
Height:	3.1m (10.17ft)
Weight:	15,000kg (33,000lb)
Ground clearance:	0.4m (1.31ft)
Armament:	none
Crew:	1
Top speed:	80km/h (50mph)
Range:	700km (438 miles)
Fording:	0.5m (1.64ft)
Gradient:	15 percent
Configuration:	6 x 6

M1070

The Heavy Equipment Transporter System (HETS) produced by the Oshkosh Truck Corporation – which consists of the M1070 truck tractor and M1000 semi-trailer – transports tanks and other heavy tracked and wheeled vehicles to and from the battlefield. The M1070 tractor and M1000 semi-trailer replaces the M911/M747 HET system as the US Army's latest model HETS. The M1070/M1000 HETS was developed to accommodate the increased weight of the M1 Abrams family of main battle tanks. The M1070 provides long-haul, local-haul and mainte-nance evacuation on- and offroad during tactical operations worldwide. Unlike previous HETS, the M1070 is designed to carry both the tank and its crew. The HETS is required to transport, deploy and evacuate 70-ton payloads, primarily M1 tanks, on highways and unimproved roads and cross-country. HETS has automatically steerable axles and load-levelling hydraulic suspension. The tractor has front and rear axle steering with a central tyre inflation system and cab space for five crew members. HETS, which was not available for service during the 1991 Gulf War, entered low-rate ini-tial production soon afterwards. At the completion of the initial contract in 1992, the US Army had purchased 1179 trucks and trailers.

SPECIFICATIONS

Type:	*heavy equipment transporter*
Manufacturer:	*Oshkosh*
Powerplant:	*Detroit Diesel 8V92TA*
Horsepower:	*500*
Transmission:	*5 + 1*
Length:	*9.19m (30.16ft)*
Width:	*2.59m (8.5ft)*
Height:	*3.73m (12.25ft)*
Weight:	*39,009kg (86,000lb)*
Ground clearance:	*0.5m (1.64ft)*
Armament:	*none*
Crew:	*5*
Top speed:	*unknown*
Range:	*520km (325 miles)*
Fording:	*0.71m (2.32ft)*
Gradient:	*15 percent*
Configuration:	*8 x 8*

M1100 WTM

Iveco was established in 1975, bringing together the commercial vehicle businesses of Fiat, OM and Lancia Veicoli Speciali in Italy; Unic in France; and Magirus-Deutz in Germany. These mergers created the first truly pan-European truck manufacturer, with a significant presence across all major European markets. In 1986, a joint venture with Ford of Britain led to the creation of Iveco Ford Truck in the United Kingdom and, in 1991, the Spanish company Pegaso and the British Seddon Atkinson joined the group. Iveco has subsequently embarked on one of the most demanding restructuring programmes ever undertaken by a commercial vehicle manufacturer. This rationalization has resulted in Iveco becoming a world leader in transport technology. Iveco Defence Vehicles Division (DVD) is one of the divisions within the Iveco organisation. Iveco DVD has a long history of success in meeting the exacting demands of the military user in the fields of both armoured fighting and logistic vehicles. The M1100 is capable of transporting the Ariete main battle tank. It is a heavy transporter with two winches, each having a pulling capacity of 25,000kg (55,000lb). The 500 horsepower engine is capable of giving the tractor a top speed of 80km/h (50mph), while the front and rear disc brakes provide excellent stopping power.

SPECIFICATIONS

Type:	tank transporter
Manufacturer:	Iveco
Powerplant:	Iveco 8460.41 diesel
Horsepower:	500
Transmission:	16 + 6
Length:	8.64m (28.34ft)
Width:	2.88m (9.44ft)
Height:	3.03m (9.94ft)
Weight:	19,000kg (41,800lb)
Ground clearance:	0.43m (1.41ft)
Armament:	none
Crew:	1
Top speed:	80km/h (50mph)
Range:	unknown
Fording:	1m (3.28ft)
Gradient:	20 percent
Configuration:	8 x 8

T144GB

To pull a trailer loaded with a main battle tank requires a large powerplant. This vehicle is powered by the Environmental class Euro 2 engine. It has a compression ratio of 17:1, maximum power of 530 horsepower at 1900rpm, maximum torque of 2300 and a recommended engine speed of 1200–1550rpm. The size of the engine is 14 litres. Scania has invested heavily in safety for the driver. For example, the seat belt is the single most important item of safety equipment for the driver. With the belt on, the seat occupant stays securely in place instead of risking being catapulted out of the cab. The company has integrated the belt with the seat so that it remains perfectly comfortable even during long stints behind the wheel. Additional protection is available in the form of a belt pre-tensioner and airbag, but for these features to be effective, the seat belt must be worn. Scania trucks feature an under-run beam in the front bumper as standard. This considerably increases the survival margin in crashes. Scania offers electronically regulated disc brakes on most models in long-haul and distribution operations. Disc brakes offer extra-high braking power and reduce the risk of brake fade, while the electronic brake regulation system increases the speed and precision of brake operation. This vehicle is in Belgian Army service.

SPECIFICATIONS

Type:	tank transporter
Manufacturer:	Scania
Powerplant:	Enviromental class Euro 2 diesel
Horsepower:	530
Transmission:	9 + 1
Length:	8.2m (26.9ft)
Width:	2.49m (8.16ft)
Height:	3.44m (11.28ft)
Weight:	38,500kg (84,700lb)
Ground clearance:	0.31m (1.01m)
Armament:	none
Crew:	1
Top speed:	80km/h (50mph)
Range:	unknown
Fording:	0.5m (1.64ft)
Gradient:	30 percent
Configuration:	6 x 4

T-815

The TATRA T815-24EN34 semi-trailer prime mover is designed to haul semi-trailers transporting tanks, armoured personnel carriers and other military loads. The 6 x 6 all-wheel drive uses the TATRA-designed suspension system – central backbone tube with swing half-axles – which is extremely resistant against torsional and bending stresses and makes it possible to negotiate difficult terrain and rough surfaces at higher speeds. It also gives better ride comfort than with a conventional chassis. This semi-trailer also incorporates airbags and leaf springs, which makes it possible to keep the fifth wheel height independent of the load. The braking system comprises dual-circuit pressure air brakes, which are load sensitive and act on the wheels of all the axles. The emergency brake is a spring type which acts on the rear axle wheels only. The vehicle has 10 forward and 2 reverse gears and, except for the first and reverse gears, all gears are synchronized. The cab is all metal with a hydraulic tilt and two doors. Inside are two full-size seats and an emergency seat which can be adapted into a berth should the need arise. The steering is left-hand drive with integral power assistance, and the clutch is single plate with a diaphragm spring.

SPECIFICATIONS

Type:	prime mover
Manufacturer:	TATRA
Powerplant:	TATRA T3B92B
Horsepower:	400
Transmission:	10 + 2
Length:	7.6m (24.93ft)
Width:	2.5m (8.2ft)
Height:	3.03m (9.94ft)
Weight:	36,000kg (79,200lb)
Ground clearance:	0.35m(1.14ft)
Armament:	none
Crew:	1
Top speed:	80km/h (50mph)
Range:	400km (250 miles)
Fording:	0.4m (1.31ft)
Gradient:	22 percent
Configuration:	6 x 6

40.10

The Iveco 40.10 light truck, currently in use with the Italian Army, has a conventional layout with the engine at the front and the cargo area at the rear. Having a payload of 1500kg (3300lb), it is ideally suited for many tactical roles such as troop and cargo carrier. The driving cab usually has a soft canvas top though a hard top is also available. The cargo compartment is of all-steel construction and has folding seats along each side for 10 men. The bonnet can be removed to allow access to the engine for routine maintenance. The truck can be configured in a number of ways. For example, a van body is available as well as a four-stretcher ambulance body. The cargo area can also house numerous weapons, such as the 106mm recoilless rifle, plus anti-tank weapons, machine guns and rocket launchers. The truck itself can tow a 105mm light artillery piece, and an optional front winch is also available. Two 40.10 trucks can be fitted inside a C-130 Hercules transport aircraft for rapid deployment, and a stripped-down one can be accommodated inside a C-223 transport aircraft. The axles are of the single reduction type front and rear, both with locking differentials. Hydraulic power steering is standard and left- and right-hand steering versions are available.

SPECIFICATIONS

Type:	*light truck*
Manufacturer:	*Iveco*
Powerplant:	*Fiat 8142 diesel*
Horsepower:	*103*
Transmission:	*5 + 1*
Length:	*4.64m (15.22ft)*
Width:	*2m (6.56ft)*
Height:	*2.38m (7.8ft)*
Weight:	*4300kg (9460lb)*
Ground clearance:	*0.4m (1.31ft)*
Armament:	*none*
Crew:	*1*
Top speed:	*100km/h (62.5mph)*
Range:	*500km (312 miles)*
Fording:	*0.7m (2.29ft)*
Gradient:	*60 percent*
Configuration:	*4 x 4*

ATMP

Supacat has been in service with the British Army since the mid-1980s as an all-terrain mobile platform. It is a fully automatic 6 x 6 airportable and amphibious vehicle, with a 1000kg (2200lb) payload and an unrivalled all-terrain capability. The Mark III version has recently been selected by Great Britain's Ministry of Defence for the British Army's 16th Air Assault Brigade as part of the All Terrain Mobile Platform (ATMP) programme. The vehicle uses a forward-controlling driving position with accommodation for a passenger next to the driver and space for a further four men in the rear if necessary. The vehicle has a limited amphibious capability and can also travel through snow. However, in arctic conditions tracks can be fitted to make transport easier – they take around 15 minutes to fit. As well as an all-terrain vehicle, it is possible that the ATMP can be used as an anti-tank and anti-aircraft missile carrier. A specially designed transporter trailer which tilts automatically for loading and off-loading is also available. The payload for the vehicle is 1000kg (2200lb), and with the trailer this increases by a further 400kg (880lb). The ATMP may be used in an all-flat bed form or with a fixed cab depending on mission requirements.

SPECIFICATIONS

Type:	*light vehicle*
Manufacturer:	*Alvis Vehicles*
Powerplant:	*VW 1.588 diesel*
Horsepower:	*54*
Transmission:	*3 + 1*
Length:	*3.14m (10.3ft)*
Width:	*2m (6.56ft)*
Height:	*2m (6.56ft)*
Weight:	*2520kg (5544lb)*
Ground clearance:	*0.24m (0.78ft)*
Armament:	*none*
Crew:	*1*
Top speed:	*48km/h (30mph)*
Range:	*unknown*
Fording:	*0.75m (2.46ft)*
Gradient:	*45 percent*
Configuration:	*6 x 6*

AWB BEDFORD

This truck was the winner of the British Army's 4 x 4000kg (8800lb) truck competition to replace the venerable Bedford RL truck. The vehicle has a ladder-type chassis with six cross-members, two being of "alligator jaw" design. The two-door forward control cab is of all-steel construction and has a circular observation hatch in the roof. Access to the engine is via the top-hinged panels on the rear of the cab at either side, and the cab between the driver's and passenger's seats is easily removed for access to the engine. The rear cargo area has drop tail-gate and sides, which can be removed easily for the stowage of containers. A hydraulic crane can be fitted for unloading, and detachable outward-facing seats can be fitted in the centre of the cargo area for the transport of passengers. This ubiquitous vehicle comes in a number of variants: dump truck, refueller and portable roadway laying vehicle. The Bedford can also be fitted with a winch, which has a capacity of 5080kg (11,176lb) and a cable length of 76m (249.3ft). The cab itself can be made mineproof, though this requires detailed work carried out by a specialist firm. Some 50,000 Bedfords have been manufactured, testimony to its robust and reliable qualities.

SPECIFICATIONS

Type:	4000kg truck
Manufacturer:	AWB Bedford
Powerplant:	Bedford 5.42 diesel
Horsepower:	98
Transmission:	4 + 1
Length:	6.57m (21.55ft)
Width:	2.48m (8.13ft)
Height:	3.4m (11.15ft)
Weight:	11,180kg (24,596lb)
Ground clearance:	0.34m (1.11ft)
Armament:	none
Crew:	1
Top speed:	77km/h (48.12mph)
Range:	560km (350 miles)
Fording:	0.76m (2.49ft)
Gradient:	49 percent
Configuration:	4 x 4

BV206

The Bv206 all-terrain carrier is a family of multipurpose amphibious tracked vehicles. The Bv206 can be found in both military and civilian applications all over the world and new categories of users appear all the time. From the earliest stage, the Bv206 was designed to be versatile and it has been proven so in service. With generous power driving on all four of the tracks, which exert a ground pressure of less than half of a man's foot, the Bv206 can negotiate such obstacles as soft snow, drifting sand and marshlands. It can climb considerable gradients, swim without preparation and work in arctic cold or in tropical heat. The load capacity is 2250kg (4950lb). A trailer of 2500kg (5500lb) gross weight can also be towed. The front and rear units are connected by a unique hydraulic steering linkage, which gives great flexibility in all axles and extremely good manoeuvrability. The simplicity in the handling of the vehicle involves a minimum of driver training. The vehicle can be airdropped and transported by a variety of aircraft and helicopters. The latest member of the Bv206 family is the improved armoured version called BvS10. The BvS10 is a new larger vehicle, with improved load capacity. The BvS10 has the same superior mobility in difficult terrain as the Bv206, combined with the same speed on road.

SPECIFICATIONS

Type:	all-terrain carrier
Manufacturer:	Hägglunds
Powerplant:	Mercedes OM 603.950
Horsepower:	136
Transmission:	4 + 1
Length:	6.9m (22.63ft)
Width:	1.87m (6.13ft)
Height:	2.3m (7.54ft)
Weight:	4500kg (9900lb)
Ground clearance:	0.35m (1.14ft)
Armament:	none
Crew:	1
Top speed:	52km/h (32.5mph)
Range:	330km (206 miles)
Fording:	amphibious
Gradient:	60 percent
Configuration:	tracked

DROPS

The Demountable Rack Offload and Pickup System (DROPS) is currently in use with the British Army. The Leyland DAF is an 8 x 6 vehicle that can carry a 15,000kg (33,000lb) payload with a mobility equivalent to a medium load, hence its name Medium Mobility Load Carrier (MMLC). It uses a forward control cab with seating for the driver and a second crew member; there is also space for a third crew member if necessary, plus space for crew stowage. A hatch with a machine-gun mounting is located in the roof (which can take the weight of two men). The vehicle uses the Multilift Mark 4 load-handling system, which was designed for offroad military applications. The control system uses automatic single lever operation with two modes of backup for emergencies. It allows the carrier vehicle not only to lift flatracks onto the carrier but also to move them on the ground. The driver controls the hook arm, which lowers and then lifts the flatrack onto the vehicle. Load and unload times are between 25 and 30 seconds. The system uses a simple chassis interface with minimum mounting points and high-quality steel throughout. All pivots and bearings are designed for ease of access, including grease seals.

SPECIFICATIONS

Type:	logistic support
Manufacturer:	Leyland DAF
Powerplant:	Eagle 350M diesel
Horsepower:	350
Transmission:	6 + 1
Length:	9.11m (29.88ft)
Width:	2.5m (8.2ft)
Height:	3.18m (10.43ft)
Weight:	32,000kg (70,400lb)
Ground clearance:	0.28m (0.91ft)
Armament:	none
Crew:	2
Top speed:	75km/h (46.87mph)
Range:	500km (312 miles)
Fording:	0.75m (2.46ft)
Gradient:	61 percent
Configuration:	8 x 6

FM12

The Volvo FM12 is a powerful, robust truck built for very demanding duties and is certified for gross combination weights of up to 100,000kg (220,000lb) in heavy construction work. The Volvo FM12 has a raised ground clearance, low-loading height, well-protected components and Powertronic or I-shift automatic gearboxes. Safety features include the Electronic Stability Programme (ESP), which activates the braking system automatically if the truck shows tendencies to abnormal behaviour. Electronically controlled disc brakes on air suspended models minimize the risk of brake fade, and a computerized driver information system with large display for driver information gives clear feedback on the truck's functions and status. Brake blending ensures that the disc brakes, retarder and/or Volvo Engine Brake interact to provide optimum braking. Driver comfort is improved by ergonomically designed and logically grouped instruments. Comfortable, air-suspended seats with adjustable damping and integrated seat belts, available with the option of built-in heating and ventilation, are also available. The cab is easy to tilt either manually or with the help of the optional electrically powered hydraulic pump. A cab tilt angle of 70 degrees allows easy access to most service components.

SPECIFICATIONS

Type:	heavy truck
Manufacturer:	Volvo
Powerplant:	D12C 420 diesel
Horsepower:	414
Transmission:	6 + 1
Length:	8.45m (27.72ft)
Width:	2.46m (8.07ft)
Height:	2.86m (9.38ft)
Weight:	35,000kg (77,000lb)
Ground clearance:	0.23m (0.75ft)
Armament:	none
Crew:	1
Top speed:	80km/h (50mph)
Range:	500km (312 miles)
Fording:	1.1m (3.6ft)
Gradient:	30 percent
Configuration:	6 x 6

HEMTT

The M977 Series of Heavy Expanded Mobility Tactical Trucks (HEMTT) is considered by many to be the world's premier heavy duty tactical truck, and was affectionately referred to as "The Ship of the Desert" during the 1991 Gulf War. The 8 x 8 HEMTT is highly valued for its ability to provide support wherever the US Army's tanks are going. Over 15,000 HEMTTs have been built and fielded since 1982, with the newest model, the HEMTT Load Handling System (LHS), now entering production to support transportation of palletized loads. The HEMTT Overhaul programme is the systematic disassembly, component rebuild and production-line truck re-assembly providing the same performance, life-span and warranty as a new HEMTT. Of the 15,000 HEMTTs built by Oshkosh, over 800 have been overhauled to date. There are five basic configurations of the HEMTT series of trucks: M977 cargo truck with Material Handling Crane (MHC), M978 2500-gallon fuel tanker, M984 wrecker, M983 tractor and M985 cargo truck with MHC. A self-recovery winch is also available on certain models. This vehicle family is rapidly deployable and is designed to operate in any climatic condition where military operations are expected to occur.

SPECIFICATIONS

Type:	*heavy truck*
Manufacturer:	*Oshkosh*
Powerplant:	*DDC Model 8V92TA*
Horsepower:	*450*
Transmission:	*4-speed automatic*
Length:	*10.17m (33.36ft)*
Width:	*2.43m (7.97ft)*
Height:	*2.56m (8.39ft)*
Weight:	*28,123kg (62,000lb)*
Ground clearance:	*0.6m (1.96ft)*
Armament:	*none*
Crew:	*1*
Top speed:	*62mph (38.75mph)*
Range:	*640km (400 miles)*
Fording:	*0.12m (0.39ft)*
Gradient:	*60 percent*
Configuration:	*8 x 8*

LAND ROVER 90

The Land Rover 90 is fitted with long-travel coil spring suspension and front disc brakes. It has a boxed-section steel chassis with a cross member bolted in place to aid removal of the gearbox and transfer box. Suspension movement is controlled at the front and the rear by long-stroke hydraulic dampers. The front beam axle is located by radius arms with Panhard rods providing lateral location. The rear axle is located by tubular trailing links with a centrally mounted A-frame. Up to three engines are available for this vehicle: 2.5-litre petrol, 3.5-litre V-8 petrol and a 2.5-litre diesel, which is available in naturally aspirated or turbocharged versions. The gearbox and transfer in the 90 is the same as those in the 110. Like all Land Rover vehicles, the 90 comes with a number of options, including open top with folding windscreen and detachable door tops, a roll-over bar, NATO standard towing jaw and 12-pin trailer socket, blackout lighting systems, small-arms clips, hand throttle, wire mesh lamp guards, raised air intake, and front and rear seating options. Land Rover vehicles are popular around the world and are manufactured in many countries, including Australia, Malaysia, Turkey, Zambia, Morocco and Zaire.

SPECIFICATIONS

Type:	*light vehicle*
Manufacturer:	*Land Rover*
Powerplant:	*V-8 petrol*
Horsepower:	*134*
Transmission:	*5 + 1*
Length:	*3.72m (12.2ft)*
Width:	*1.79m (5.87ft)*
Height:	*1.99m (6.52ft)*
Weight:	*2550kg (5610lb)*
Ground clearance:	*0.21m (0.68ft)*
Armament:	*depends on variant*
Crew:	*1*
Top speed:	*105km/h (65.62mph)*
Range:	*600km (375 miles)*
Fording:	*0.5m (1.64ft)*
Gradient:	*39 percent*
Configuration:	*4 x 4*

LAND ROVER 110

The 110 is based on a box-section steel chassis used on the civilian Range Rover, though considerably strengthened. This strength has been incorporated to allow the vehicle to withstand the most demanding offroad conditions. The suspension uses coil springs in place of the earlier leaf-spring type. The military version of the 110 is in service with the British Army and is known by the designation Truck, Utility, Medium. A wide range of conversions have been developed for this vehicle, including a special forces patrol vehicle, armoured patrol vehicle, mobile workshops, shelter vehicles, ambulances, towlift recovery vehicles and a hydraulically operated multi-loader. Weapons fit depends on the version, but can include MILAN anti-tank rocket launcher, 70mm multiple rocket system and 7.62mm machine guns. Factory fitted options include truck cab, open top with folding windscreen and detachable door tops, rollover bar, additional fuel tanks, air conditioning, small-arms clips, wire mesh lamp guards, disruptive-pattern camouflage paint, cabinets for jerry can stowage, and external pick and shovel stowage. The popularity of Land Rover vehicles stems from their versatility, ruggedness and ease of maintenance in the field, which often involves nothing more than work with a hammer and screwdriver.

SPECIFICATIONS

Type:	lightweight vehicle
Manufacturer:	Land Rover
Powerplant:	V-8 watercooled petrol
Horsepower:	134
Transmission:	5 + 1
Length:	4.63m (15.19ft)
Width:	1.79m (5.87ft)
Height:	1.03m (3.37ft)
Weight:	3050kg (6710lb)
Ground clearance:	0.21m (0.68ft)
Armament:	depends on variant
Crew:	1
Top speed:	105km/h (65.62mph)
Range:	600km (375 miles)
Fording:	0.7m (2.29ft)
Gradient:	40 percent
Configuration:	4 x 4

LEYLAND DAF

Currently in service with the British Army following the award by the Ministry of Defence of a production contract to Leyland DAF in 1989, this truck is conventional in both layout and design. The sleeper cab has room for the driver, two passengers and stowage for their kit. Alternatively, the space can be used for driver training or radio communications equipment depending on the requirement. The cab roof itself is strengthened to bear the weight of two men and has provision for a roof hatch and machine-gun installation over an observer's platform inside the cab. There are a number of fitments that can be added to the truck, including front-end rotating hooks, lugs for suspended or supported recovery and an infrared reflective paint finish. The body has been designed to accommodate interchangeable drop sides, a tailboard and canopy. Options include left- or right-hand drive, a winch, hydraulic crane, tipping body or a chassis-and-cab-only arrangement. The front axle has a rating of 4850kg (10,670lb) with an off-set bowl to reduce cab height, and the rear axle has a rating of 6800kg (14,960lb). The vehicle can accommodate numerous items of military equipment, such as NATO-standard pallets, containers and fuel pods.

SPECIFICATIONS

Type:	medium truck
Manufacturer:	Leyland DAF
Powerplant:	Leyland DAF 310 diesel
Horsepower:	145
Transmission:	5 + 1
Length:	6.65m (21.81ft)
Width:	2.49m (8.16ft)
Height:	3.43m (11.25ft)
Weight:	10,800kg (23,760lb)
Ground clearance:	0.32m (1.04ft)
Armament:	none
Crew:	1
Top speed:	89km/h (55.62mph)
Range:	500km (312 miles)
Fording:	0.75m (2.46ft)
Gradient:	33 percent
Configuration:	4 x 4

M115.18WM

The success Iveco has enjoyed is due to a process of continuous product evolution, which means that the specification and choice of models are always being changed to meet the needs of military customers. The latest evolution is the range of medium trucks. The M115 has been designed to be more responsive, more reliable and more profitable for customers. In addition to boasting the pedigree of a truck that has already won more awards than any other, it has now been equipped with a new engine offering even higher standards of productivity. The new Tector engine has been designed specifically for the EuroCargo by Iveco, one of the world's largest manufacturers of truck diesel engines. The new Tector engine family is in fact the latest in a generation of leading edge engines, specifically designed by Iveco. The advent of the unprecedented "common rail" direct injection diesel turbo engines with four valves per cylinder and integrated intake manifold offers new levels of reliability, long-term durability and low impact on the environment. The fascia is ergonomical, the instrumentation is housed in an anti-glare dashboard, and the main controls are on the three steering column stalks. The large side windows, extending below the waistline, provide excellent kerbside vision.

SPECIFICATIONS

Type:	*medium truck*
Manufacturer:	*Iveco*
Powerplant:	*Iveco Tector diesel*
Horsepower:	*177*
Transmission:	*6 + 1*
Length:	*6.96m (22.83ft)*
Width:	*2.48m (8.13ft)*
Height:	*3.07m (10.07ft)*
Weight:	*12,400kg (27,280ft)*
Ground clearance:	*0.43m (1.41ft)*
Armament:	*none*
Crew:	*1*
Top speed:	*80km/h (50mph)*
Range:	*500km (312 miles)*
Fording:	*unknown*
Gradient:	*60 percent*
Configuration:	*4 x 4*

M150.30WM

esides vehicle performance, cost effective logistic and after-sales support are key drivers in Iveco's design philosophy for military customers. Maximum use of commercial off-the-shelf components with proven reliability contributes to lower life-cycle costs as well as minimizing the cost of replacement parts. Computerized diagnostic systems for maintenance and fleet management are provided, essential tools for ensuring long and efficient vehicle life. Iveco fits a number of useful features into its machines. For example, fully electronic engine management is by means of an engine control unit (ECU) fitted directly to the engine via a connecting plate in which fuel is circulated to cool it down. To facilitate diagnostic tasks, the ECU memorizes several operating parameters, such as coolant temperature, oil temperature and pressure, as well as any instance of malfunctioning. In the event of a failure, Iveco has designed a feature that facilitates return to base: the computer will see to the engine's "self-defence" by activating a "limp-home" programme that makes it possible to keep working with downgraded performance capabilities. If necessary, the data saved can be transmitted to the Iveco service network via a cable or via the telecommunications lines.

SPECIFICATIONS

Type:	heavy truck
Manufacturer:	Iveco
Powerplant:	Iveco CURSOR 8 diesel
Horsepower:	221
Transmission:	16 + 16 or 5 + 5
Length:	7.87m (25.82ft)
Width:	2.5m (8.2ft)
Height:	3m (9.84ft)
Weight:	17,000kg (37,400lb)
Ground clearance:	0.43m (1.41ft)
Armament:	none
Crew:	1
Top speed:	90km/h (56.25mph)
Range:	500km (312 miles)
Fording:	unknown
Gradient:	60 percent
Configuration:	4 x 4

M250.37WM

The cab of the M250 is modelled on the civilian road versions of the model; it therefore offers the driver a comfortable and ergonomic working environment. Iveco has invested a lot of time and money in cab design, and that's why the EuroTrakker Cursor results in an even more comfortable cab, in which insulation has been improved by 20 percent and soundproofing has been reduced. Working in difficult conditions is no longer a problem, the Eurotrakker Cursor uses a new cab suspension system, capable of isolating the driver from the ruggedness of the terrain and of softening rolling on bends, giving greater driving comfort. What's more, to ensure value is retained over time, the cab panels are galvanized on both sides. This guarantees greater protection and durability for the driver compartment. Like the rest of their military range, this vehicle is powered by an Iveco engine. Four million engines currently operate on various types of machine, from the simplest to the most complex, guaranteeing customers a high level of reliability and durability that is the outcome of Iveco's long tradition in engine production. Iveco engines are ideal for the military market because they have long intervals between overhauls. This means that they can support military operations for extended lengths of time.

SPECIFICATIONS

Type:	*heavy truck*
Manufacturer:	*Iveco*
Powerplant:	*Iveco 8460.41 diesel*
Horsepower:	*272*
Transmission:	*6 + 6*
Length:	*8.59m (28.18ft)*
Width:	*2.5m (8.2ft)*
Height:	*3m (9.84ft)*
Weight:	*25,000kg (55,000lb)*
Ground clearance:	*0.43m (1.41ft)*
Armament:	*none*
Crew:	*1*
Top speed:	*90km/h (56.25mph)*
Range:	*500km (312 miles)*
Fording:	*unknown*
Gradient:	*60 percent*
Configuration:	*6 x 6*

M320.42WM

Like most Iveco transport vehicles, the M320 uses ABS as standard and the front axles of partial drive versions are equipped with disc brakes, while the drive axles are equipped with drum brakes. Some of the advantages of the front disc brakes are: balancing of brake power (left and right), rapid reaction times, and quick and easy substitution of brake pads. All of this means an increase in safety and a reduction in operating costs. The efficiency of the brake system is improved by not only the ABS system, but also the EBL (Electronic Braking Limitation) system, an electronic braking corrector integrated into the ABS system, which requires no servicing interventions at all. The Air Processing Unit (APU) system also adds to the reliability of the brake system components as it improves the air-drying process through an air heating and filtering system which feeds the whole pneumatic system. Iveco supplies the Italian Army with its range of trucks, and also the Ariete main battle tank. Like most Iveco vehicles, the M320 is C-130 transportable and the cab area is easily armoured with the addition of appliqué panels. This means that the vehicle can withstand hits from small-arms fire and artillery fragments, thereby allowing it to operate near the frontline if necessary.

SPECIFICATIONS

Type:	heavy truck
Manufacturer:	Iveco
Powerplant:	Iveco CURSOR 10 diesel
Horsepower:	420
Transmission:	6 + 6
Length:	10.15m (33.3ft)
Width:	2.5m (8.2ft)
Height:	3.34m (10.95ft)
Weight:	32,000kg (70,400lb)
Ground clearance:	0.43m (1.41ft)
Armament:	none
Crew:	1
Top speed:	90km/h (56.25mph)
Range:	450km (281 miles)
Fording:	unknown
Gradient:	60
Configuration:	8 x 8

M809

The M809 series of trucks in service with the US Army is similar to the older M54 series, with a diesel engine fitted in place of the multi-fuel powerplant of the earlier model. Production of the M809 started in 1970 and by the mid-1980s AM General had built 38,000 vehicles. The chassis consists of two rail-type beams with six reinforced cross-members. The layout of the truck is conventional: the engine at the front, a two-door cab in the centre with a windscreen that can be folded flat against the bonnet, a removable canvas top and a cargo compartment at the rear. The basic cargo variant has an all-steel rear cargo body with drop sides, removable bows, tarpaulin cover and troop seats down either side for up to 18 fully equipped troops. A number of extras are available for this vehicle, including A-frame, air brakes, closure hard-top, deep water fording, thermal barrier and water personnel heater. In addition, a winch can be fitted at the front. The trucks can also be fitted with the Enhanced Mobility System for increased mobility over sand, snow and mud. The truck is in the service of the US Army and several other armed forces around the world, including Jordan, South Korea, Pakistan and Thailand. As can be seen in the photograph, equipment can also be stashed on the cab roof.

SPECIFICATIONS

Type:	cargo truck
Manufacturer:	AM General
Powerplant:	NHC-250 diesel
Horsepower:	240
Transmission:	5 + 1
Length:	7.65m (25.09ft)
Width:	2.46m (8.07ft)
Height:	2.94m (8.16ft)
Weight:	18,985kg (41,767lb)
Ground clearance:	0.29m (0.95ft)
Armament:	none
Crew:	1
Top speed:	84km/h (52.5mph)
Range:	563km (352 miles)
Fording:	0.76m (2.49ft)
Gradient:	67 percent
Configuration:	6 x 6

M923

The M923 is a dropside version of the venerable M939 series of 6 x 6 cargo trucks in US service. The truck has a fully automatic transmission that eliminates over-revving, is very reliable, easy to operate and features improvements in overall safety. For example, the driver controls the engagement of the front wheels for 6 x 6 drive with an air system, which eliminates the need for a mechanical sprague clutch, which often failed. The truck is equipped with air brakes, which are self-adjusting and are backed by fail-safe mechanical spring brakes. The front-mounted winch is hydraulically driven and stops when overloaded and restarts when the overload is removed. The bonnet and bumpers tilt forward to allow maintenance to be carried out from ground level. Flat tyres are replaced using a boom positioned just behind the cab. In April 1981 the AM Corporation was awarded a contract for 11,394 M939s, later increased to 22,789. AM General completed its five-year contract in September 1986, though production was extended until April 1987 by the award of a further contract for 1107 vehicles. As a result of this large production run the M939 series is in widespread use. There is no doubt that this series of trucks has been the backbone of the US Army for over 20 years.

SPECIFICATIONS

Type:	cargo truck
Manufacturer:	AM General
Powerplant:	Cummins NHC-250 diesel
Horsepower:	240
Transmission:	5 + 1
Length:	7.74m (25.39ft)
Width:	2.46m (8.07ft)
Height:	2.94m (9.64ft)
Weight:	9797kg (21,553lb)
Ground clearance:	0.27m (0.88ft)
Armament:	none
Crew:	1
Top speed:	84km/h (52.5mph)
Range:	563km (352 miles)
Fording:	0.76m (2.49ft)
Gradient:	60 percent
Configuration:	6 x 6

M939A2

The story of this vehicle begins with the earlier M809 series of 6 x 6 trucks that was developed and produced by the AM General Corporation. Production began in 1970, and by mid-1980 some 38,000 vehicles had been completed. The company announced in 1988 that it was withdrawing from the manufacture of medium and heavy vehicles. However, the US Army awarded an engineering contract to AM General for the further development of the M809, which resulted in the M939. In April 1979 AM was awarded a contract for 11,394 M939s, later increased to 22,789. In May 1986 ARVECO, a joint venture between BMY Corporation and the General Automative Company, was awarded a contract to build 15,218 M939A2s over a five-year period. The first deliveries were made in early 1987. The M939 is essentially the M809 with improved transmission, transfer case and braking system. The M939A2 incorporates a central tyre inflation system. The powerplant is the Cummins engine producing 240 horsepower at 2100 revolutions per minute and giving the vehicle a range of 644km (402 miles). There are a number of kits for the M939 series, including automatic chemical alarm, deep water fording, bow and tarpaulin cover, electric brake, engine coolant heater and hard-top closure.

SPECIFICATIONS

Type:	cargo truck
Manufacturer:	BMY Division of HARSCO
Powerplant:	Cummins NHC-250 diesel
Horsepower:	240
Transmission:	5 + 1
Length:	7.74m (25.39ft)
Width:	2.46m (8.07ft)
Height:	2.94m (9.64ft)
Weight:	9797kg (21,553lb)
Ground clearance:	0.27m (0.88ft)
Armament:	none
Crew:	1
Top speed:	84km/h (52.5mph)
Range:	644km (402 miles)
Fording:	0.76m (2.49ft)
Gradient:	60 percent
Configuration:	6 x 6

M998

The High Mobility Multi-purpose Wheeled Vehicle (HMMWV) is the replacement vehicle for the M151 series of jeeps. Its mission is to provide a light tactical vehicle for command and control, special-purpose shelter carriers, and special-purpose weapons platforms throughout all areas of the modern battlefield. It is supported using the current logistics and maintenance structure established for US Army wheeled vehicles. The HMMWV is equipped with a high-performance diesel engine, automatic transmission and four wheel drive and is air transportable and droppable from a variety of aircraft. The HMMWV can be equipped with a self-recovery winch and can support payloads from 1136kg to 2000kg (2500lb to 4400lb) depending on the model. The family includes utility/cargo, shelter carrier, armament carrier, ambulance, anti-tank missile carrier and scout reconnaissance configuration. A basic armour package is standard on the Armament and anti-tank missile carrier models. A more heavily armoured, or Up-Armour, HMMWV is now being produced in limited quantities, primarily for the Scout Platoon application. Special supplemental armour versions have been developed for USMC requirements (unique model numbers designate these configurations).

SPECIFICATIONS

Type:	*utility vehicle*
Manufacturer:	*AM General*
Powerplant:	*V8, 6.2 litre diesel*
Horsepower:	*150*
Transmission:	*3-speed automatic*
Length:	*4.57m (14.99ft)*
Width:	*2.16m (7.08ft)*
Height:	*1.83m (6ft)*
Weight:	*2363kg (5200lb)*
Ground clearance:	*0.4m (1.33ft)*
Armament:	*depends on configuration*
Crew:	*2–4*
Top speed:	*88km/h (55mph)*
Range:	*560km (350 miles)*
Fording:	*0.76m (2.5ft)*
Gradient:	*60 percent*
Configuration:	*4 x 4*

M1078

Stewart & Stevenson Tactical Vehicle Systems, LP (TVSLP), a segment of Stewart & Stevenson Services, Inc. (NASDAQ: SSSS), is the manufacturer and prime contractor of the Family of Medium Tactical Vehicles (FMTV) for the US Army. The M1078 Standard Cargo Truck is designed to transport cargo and soldiers. The M1078 has a payload capacity of 2272kg (5000lb), and to facilitate loading/unloading the bed-side rails are mounted on hinges and can be lowered. The cargo bed can be equipped with an optional bench seat kit for the transport of soldiers. The bench seats are constructed of a non-wood material and attach to the cargo bed side rails, and can be folded down and stowed when not in use. Soldiers are assisted when climbing in and out of the cargo bed area with the aid of a ladder, which is stowed on the vehicle when not in use. A canvas and bows kit is available to keep both soldiers and cargo protected from the elements. The M1078 can be equipped with an optional electrically operated self-recovery winch kit capable of fore and aft vehicle recovery operations. The winch has a lift capacity of 682kg (1500lb). The winch has 93.87m (308ft) of line capacity and 4545kg (10,000lb) bare drum line pull at 110 percent overload.

SPECIFICATIONS

Type:	*medium truck*
Manufacturer:	*Stewart & Stevenson*
Powerplant:	*Caterpillar, 6.6l diesel*
Horsepower:	*225*
Transmission:	*7-speed automatic*
Length:	*6.42m (21ft)*
Width:	*2.43m (7.97ft)*
Height:	*2.84m (9.31ft)*
Weight:	*7484kg (16,465lb)*
Ground clearance:	*0.55m (1.8ft)*
Armament:	*none*
Crew:	*1*
Top speed:	*94km/h (58.75mph)*
Range:	*645km (403 miles)*
Fording:	*0.91m (2.98ft)*
Gradient:	*60 percent*
Configuration:	*4 x 4*

M1079

The Family of Medium Tactical Vehicles (FMTVs) was first produced and fielded to US Army units in 1996. This family of vehicles was designed to improve upon and replace the ageing fleet of medium tactical vehicles. The FMTVs are based on a common truck cab and chassis. The Light Medium Tactical Vehicle (LMTV) designates the 2-tonne payload capacity models consisting of cargo, airdrop cargo, and van models. The Medium Tactical Vehicle (MTV) designates the 5-ton payload capacity models consisting of cargo with and without Material Handling Equipment (MHE), airdrop cargo, long wheelbase cargo with and without MHE, tractor, wrecker, dump and airdrop dump. The M1079 van is designed to be used as a mobile shop by Direct Support Unit Maintenance contact teams. The M1079 van body is constructed of aluminium and is equipped with three double-paned windows, blackout shields, double rear doors, removable steps, and an AC/DC electrical junction box and multiple outlets. The van body can be equipped with heater and/or air conditioner. The M1079 can be equipped with a self-recovery winch kit capable of fore and aft vehicle recovery operations. It has the same characteristics as the M1078 truck's winch (see page 77).

SPECIFICATIONS

Type:	medium van
Manufacturer:	Stewart & Stevenson
Powerplant:	Caterpillar 6.6-litre diesel
Horsepower:	225
Transmission:	7-speed automatic
Length:	6.7m (21.98ft)
Width:	2.43m (7.97ft)
Height:	3.48m (11.41ft)
Weight:	8156kg (17,943lb)
Ground clearance:	0.55m (1.8ft)
Armament:	none
Crew:	1
Top speed:	94km/h (58.75mph)
Range:	645km (403 miles)
Fording:	0.91m (2.98ft)
Gradient:	60 percent
Configuration:	4 x 4

M1085

Deployability, maintainability, versatility, mobility and agility are some of the words that describe the US Army's transformation. They're also words that describe the FMTV, a critical enabler for the US Army's future vision of a more deployable and lethal combat force. The M1085 Long Wheel Base (LWB) Truck is designed to transport soldiers and cargo in International Standardized Operations Containers. The M1085 has a payload capacity of 4545kg (10,000lb) and to facilitate loading/unloading, the bed side rails are mounted on hinges. The cargo bed can be equipped with an optional bench seat kit for transport of soldiers. The bench seats are constructed of a non-wood material and attach to the cargo bed side rails. The seats can be folded down and stowed when not in use. Soldier-requested improvements have been incorporated into the A1 models, such as more ergonomic and stronger grab-bars for easier cab entry, increased protection against brush damage to a variety of external components, and reinforced rear light carriers. The FMTV series incorporates a new, more powerful engine that meets the more stringent United States Environment Protection Agency emissions standards and delivers up to a 22 percent increase in horsepower and up to a 28 percent increase in torque.

SPECIFICATIONS

Type:	medium truck
Manufacturer:	Stewart & Stevenson
Powerplant:	Caterpillar 6.6-litre diesel
Horsepower:	290
Transmission:	7-speed automatic
Length:	8.86m (29.06ft)
Width:	2.43m (7.97ft)
Height:	2.84m (9.31ft)
Weight	9451kg (20,792lb)
Ground clearance:	0.55m (1.8ft)
Armament:	none
Crew:	1
Top speed:	94km/h (58.75mph)
Range:	645km (403 miles)
Fording:	0.91m (2.98ft)
Gradient:	60 percent
Configuration:	4 x 4

M1093

The FMTV brings state-of-the-art commercial truck technology to military tactical vehicles with an Anti-Lock Braking System on both the trucks and companion trailers, including an exhaust retarder, a Central Tire Inflation System (CTIS) for changing terrains, and an ultra high-speed J1939 electronic Databus. This Databus makes the new Interactive Electronic Technical Manual, or IETM, possible. This Class 5 IETM – the most advanced on the market – with intrusive diagnostics plugs into the central nervous system of the vehicle and interactively works with the vehicle's four separate electronic control units. Utilizing the highest resolution available, the IETM identifies vehicle problems and solutions, calls out necessary tools and hardware and provides detailed repair instructions – increasing overall efficiency and accuracy of maintenance tasks. The M1093 Standard Cargo Truck is designed to be loaded on and dropped from C-130 aircraft into remote areas where landing strips are not available. The vehicle is equipped to transport cargo and soldiers, as required. The M1093 has a payload capacity of 4545kg (10,000lb) and to facilitate loading/unloading of cargo, the bed side rails are mounted on hinges.

SPECIFICATIONS

Type:	cargo truck
Manufacturer:	Stewart & Stevenson
Powerplant:	Caterpillar 6.6-litre diesel
Horsepower:	290
Transmission:	7-speed automatic
Length:	6.93m (22.73ft)
Width:	2.43m (7.97ft)
Height:	2.84m (9.31ft)
Weight:	9498kg (20,896lb)
Ground clearance:	0.55m (1.8ft)
Armament:	none
Crew:	1
Top speed:	94km/h (58.75mph)
Range:	483km (302 miles)
Fording:	0.91m (2.98ft)
Gradient:	60 percent
Configuration:	6 x 6

MTVR

The US Marine Corps' Medium Tactical Vehicle Replacement (MTVR) offers a revolution in offroad mobility. With the Oshkosh Modular Independent Suspension (OMIS) system, the MTVR achieves levels of performance never before realized in a tactical wheeled vehicle, enabling the MTVR to traverse terrain previously regarded as impassable by trucks. The truck utilizes the latest in technological advancements, including IDS (independent suspension), auto-traction control and anti-lock braking systems. Long and short wheel base cargoes are currently in production, with dump, wrecker and other variants to be added. It can run with any ground-based military vehicle in US service, including M1 main battle tanks. The TAK-4 independent suspension system assures good handling, both on and off road, better traction, more upright stability, higher ground clearance and better suspension durability. In addition, it provides better overall vehicle durability because it filters out high frequency, low-amplitude vibrations that shake vehicle components loose. The MTVR can tow up to 10,000kg (22,000lb), such as a field howitzer or a full load of ammunition. It can also be transported by air in the fuselage of a C-130 Hercules transport aircraft or slung under a CH-53 helicopter.

SPECIFICATIONS

Type:	*medium truck*
Manufacturer:	*Oshkosh*
Powerplant:	*Caterpillar C12*
Horsepower:	*425*
Transmission:	*7 + 1*
Length:	*8m (26.24ft)*
Width:	*2.48m (8.13ft)*
Height:	*3.58m (11.74ft)*
Weight:	*28,214kg (62,070lb)*
Ground clearance:	*0.42m (1.37ft)*
Armament:	*none*
Crew:	*1*
Top speed:	*105km/h (65.62mph)*
Range:	*483km (302 miles)*
Fording:	*1.5m (4.9ft)*
Gradient:	*60 percent*
Configuration:	*6 x 6*

P114CB 6 X 6

Good overall operating economy is the result of a number of different factors, including purchase price and low running costs. This means low fuel consumption, good reliability, a long service life and simple maintenance – crucial to military operations. All Scania trucks are built on the basis of these requirements. Scania manufactures trucks for civilian and defence purposes, and is among the leaders when it comes to engineering, operational dependability and economy, a fact clearly borne out by the number of Scanias in military service around the world. Scania policy is to use standard commercial components also for defence applications. This has major advantages in terms of tailor-made specification, simplified part stockage training and servicing. As the company views it, an automotive manufacturer can derive decided advantages from developing and producing both civilian and defence trucks. For example, what is learnt on the civilian side can be turned to account when building defence vehicles and vice versa. The end result is Scania products displaying high performance, optimal economy and long service life. By drawing on a large number of standardized modules the company can build a large number of truck models and variants.

SPECIFICATIONS

Type:	heavy truck
Manufacturer:	Scania
Powerplant:	DC11 diesel
Horsepower:	340
Transmission:	automatic
Length:	7.3m (23.95ft)
Width:	2.43m (7.97ft)
Height:	3.3m (10.82ft)
Weight:	29,500kg (64,900lb)
Ground clearance:	0.4m (1.31ft)
Armament:	none
Crew:	1
Top speed:	105km/h (65.62mph)
Range:	600km (375 miles)
Fording:	0.8m (2.62ft)
Gradient:	40 percent
Configuration:	6 x 6

P124CB 6 X 6

This versatile truck is now in Swedish service. In February 2000 Scania signed an agreement with the Swedish Defence Materiel Administration for the supply of heavy trucks to the armed forces of that country. Up to 200 trucks will be delivered, and the Administration has an option to order additional trucks for delivery at a later date. The deal is the latest example of Scania being an important supplier to military customers. The vehicles, which are adapted for military duty, are fully based on Scania's civilian product concept. This gives access to the whole range of civilian parts and components, as well as Scania's service network. This has a positive effect, not least in terms of operating and maintenance costs. The majority of trucks are Scania P124 CB 6x6 with all-wheel-drive. The Multilift swap-body from HIAB Sverige AB will be fitted by Zetterbergs Produkt AB once the trucks have been delivered. Some of the trucks intended for international peacekeeping tasks have extra equipment such as additional protection for the cab, including mine shields. The P124 offers low running costs, low fuel consumption, good reliability, a long service life and simple maintenance. The truck in the picture is carrying two BV206 vehicles.

SPECIFICATIONS

Type:	*hooklift*
Manufacturer:	*Scania*
Powerplant:	*DSC 12 diesel*
Horsepower:	*360*
Transmission:	*automatic*
Length:	*9.04m (29.65ft)*
Width:	*2.34m (7.67ft)*
Height:	*3.34m (10.95ft)*
Weight:	*28,000kg (61,600lb)*
Ground clearance:	*0.4m (1.31ft)*
Armament:	*none*
Crew:	*1*
Top speed:	*105km/h (65.62mph)*
Range:	*500km (312 miles)*
Fording:	*0.8m (2.62ft)*
Gradient:	*40 percent*
Configuration:	*6 x 6*

P124CB 8 X 8

This is an an eight-wheel-drive off-road vehicle based on the company's modular system of standard components. The new truck had its premiere public showing at the leading military trade fair, Eurosatory in Paris, in 2000. The first customer to sign an order was FMV, the Swedish Defence Materiel Administration, which has placed an initial order for nine of the new trucks. They are part of a larger FMV order of just over 200 vehicles. The nine FMV trucks are all powered by the 420-horsepower Scania 12-litre engine. Although the first customer to sign an order was from the military, Scania's engineers see a variety of civilian application areas for a four-axle, all-wheel drive truck, for example as a tipper in particularly demanding operating conditions. In military guise, the emphasis is on robust resources for heavy off-road haulage duties. Scania's military vehicles are based on the company's civilian product range, which means that the entire civilian component range and parts-supply system is fully available, as well as Scania's global service network, which currently encompasses 1500 workshops in about 100 countries. This has a positive effect on operating and maintenance costs, and makes Scania's trucks attractive to potential customers, especially those in the developing world with limited budgets.

SPECIFICATIONS

Type:	off-road truck
Manufacturer:	Scania
Powerplant:	Scania Euro 2 diesel
Horsepower:	420
Transmission:	automatic
Length:	9.42m (30.9ft)
Width:	2.66m (8.72ft)
Height:	3.34m (10.95ft)
Weight:	34,000kg (74,800lb)
Ground clearance:	0.4m (1.31ft)
Armament:	none
Crew:	1
Top speed:	90km/h (56.25mph)
Range:	500km (312 miles)
Fording:	0.8m (2.62ft)
Gradient:	40 percent
Configuration:	8 x 8

PINZGAUER

The Pinzgauer range of all-terrain vehicles was developed by Steyr-Daimler-Puch as the successor to the Haflinger range of 4 x 4 vehicles. The 4 x 4 is available in two types of body: fully enclosed or with a military type body. The former has an all-steel, fully enclosed body with two doors each side and a single door at the rear. The military type body has a single door each side for the driver and one passenger. The tops of the doors can be removed, the windscreen folded down onto the bonnet, and the rear cargo area has removable bows and a tarpaulin cover. The chassis consists of a torsion resistant central tube with independent swing axles incorporating the transfer case and axle drive. The drive shaft is to the front and rear differentials are within the central tube chassis. This versatile vehicle can be fitted with optional equipment, including antenna holder, camouflage net holders, convoy lights, blackout blinds, divided windscreen, jerrycan holders, rear mounting trays, rifle holders, mounting points for shovels, rear tow hook and split battery system. A number in Austrian Army service have been fitted with 20mm anti-aircraft guns at the rear, with spare drum magazines stowed to the immediate rear of the driver's position. The Pinzgauer first entered military service, with Austria, in 1973.

SPECIFICATIONS

Type:	*all-terrain vehicle*
Manufacturer:	*Steyr-Daimler-Puch*
Powerplant:	*Steyr air-cooled petrol*
Horsepower:	*87*
Transmission:	*5 + 1*
Length:	*4.17m (13.68ft)*
Width:	*1.76m (5.77ft)*
Height:	*2m (6.56ft)*
Weight:	*2100kg (4620lb)*
Ground clearance:	*0.33m (1.08ft)*
Armament:	*none*
Crew:	*1*
Top speed:	*110km/h (68.75mph)*
Range:	*600km (375 miles)*
Fording:	*0.7m (2.29ft)*
Gradient:	*80 percent*
Configuration:	*4 x 4*

PLS

The Palletized Load System (PLS) is composed of a prime mover truck with integral self-loading and unloading transport capability, a trailer and demountable cargo beds (flatracks). The vehicle can also be equipped with materiel handling equipment and/or a winch. PLS is a key transportation component of the ammunition distribution system and can perform long-range hauling, local hauling and unit resupply of ammunition. The PLS tactical truck is a five-axle, 10-wheel drive vehicle equipped with a 500 horsepower Detroit Diesel engine, Allison automatic transmission and Central Tire Inflation System (CTIS). This combination provides a highly mobile system capable of transporting its payload in virtually any type of terrain, in any type of weather, and maintaining pace with the self-propelled artillery systems that it supports. The PLS comes in two mission oriented configurations: the M1074 and the M1075. The M1074 is equipped with a variable reach Material Handling Crane (MHC) to support forward deployed field artillery units. The M1075 is used in conjunction with the M1076 trailer but does not have the MHC. Ammunition can be loaded onto flatracks at depots, transported via container ship to theatre, picked up by the PLS truck and carried forward to line units.

SPECIFICATIONS

Type:	heavy truck and trailer
Manufacturer:	Oshkosh
Powerplant:	Detroit Diesel Model 8V92TA
Horsepower:	500
Transmission:	5 + 1
Length:	10.67m (35ft)
Width:	2.43m (7.97ft)
Height:	3.28m (10.76ft)
Weight:	39,916kg (87,815lb)
Ground clearance:	unknown
Armament:	none
Crew:	1
Top speed:	91km/h (56.87mph)
Range:	1000km (625 miles)
Fording:	1.21m (3.97ft)
Gradient:	60 percent
Configuration:	10 x 10

RB-44

This truck can be used for a variety of roles, such as troop carrier, towing a 105mm artillery piece or mounting an anti-tank missile system. The vehicle has a ladder-type bolted chassis which can accommodate various types of body. The cab is a standard three-seat type, but a conversion for carrying extra personnel and equipment is also available depending on mission requirements. The suspension system employs conventional semi-elliptical springs, fitted with double-acting telescopic shock absorbers. The brakes are vacuum-assisted with a dual-servo split system, and fitted front and rear. The front and rear axles have hypo gearing with a ratio of 4.1 to 1. The front axle's plated capacity is 2500kg (5500lb) and that of the rear 2800kg (6160lb). Variants of the vehicle include general service cargo body, soft and hard top bodies and an ambulance body. The front-mounted winch can be added to any version. The vehicle comes in three wheelbase lengths. The RB-44 was one of two final contenders for the British Army's 2-ton Truck Universal Heavy requirement, and was selected as the winner in mid-1988. The initial order was for 1000 vehicles, but the final figure was nearly double this. The RB-44 entered British Army service in 1989.

SPECIFICATIONS

Type:	*medium truck*
Manufacturer:	*Reynolds Boughton*
Powerplant:	*Perkins 110T diesel*
Horsepower:	*109*
Transmission:	*5 + 1*
Length:	*6.03m (19.78ft)*
Width:	*2.1m (6.88ft)*
Height:	*2.35m (7.7ft)*
Weight:	*5300kg (11,660lb)*
Ground clearance:	*0.3m (0.98ft)*
Armament:	*none*
Crew:	*1*
Top speed:	*109km/h (68.12mph)*
Range:	*500km (312 miles)*
Fording:	*0.75m (2.46ft)*
Gradient:	*33 percent*
Configuration:	*4 x 4*

T815-21

This truck is an offroad vehicle which has the ability to negotiate difficult terrain. Designed as a cargo or troop carrier, it has all-wheel drive and a front axle whose drive can be disconnected. In addition, it features axle and inter-axle differential locks and a central tyre inflation system. The truck has the TATRA suspension system. This features a rigid central "backbone" tube, with no torsion or bending of the chassis or superstructure. The result is a safe and trouble-free transport of sensitive loads, a high ride comfort, a faster drive offroad and a longer chassis life. All drive line shafts and other components are covered and protected inside the "backbone" tube, and each wheel moves up and down independently. This means that the vehicle can achieve higher speeds on rough roads, can traverse obstacles more easily, has excellent offroad mobility, and can absorb shocks and vibrations caused by rugged surfaces. Also, the swing half-axles are extremely resistant against impacts and shocks. TATRA has ensured a modular design for its axles, which means there is a high degree of commonality between its commercial and military models. The rear axle is sprung by the TATRA combination suspension airbags with coil springs inside, located above the central backbone.

SPECIFICATIONS

Type:	cargo truck
Manufacturer:	TATRA
Powerplant:	TATRA T3B-928
Horsepower:	450
Transmission:	10 + 2
Length:	6.88m (22.57ft)
Width:	2.6m (8.53ft)
Height:	2.99m (9.8ft)
Weight:	14,100kg (31,020lb)
Ground clearance:	0.36m (1.18ft)
Armament:	none
Crew:	1
Top speed:	120km/h (75mph)
Range:	1000km (625 miles)
Fording:	1.2m (3.93ft)
Gradient:	60 percent
Configuration:	4 x 4

T815-21VV25

TATRA produce all-round-drive vehicles with axle configurations of 4 x 4, 6 x 6, 8 x 8 and independent suspension of half-axles (TATRA chassis design concept). These vehicles provide excellent vibration attenuation and high operation speed on poor-quality roads. Tested in an extensive spectrum of operation conditions, provided with axle and inter-axle differential locks to go through the most adverse terrain, and with power trains protected against damage, these vehicles are rugged. They have a high-rigidity load-carrying structure, resulting in minimum longitudinal distortion, in contrast to traditional chassis found on other vehicles. Like all TATRA trucks, this vehicle has dual-circuit pressure air brakes acting on all wheels. The cab is all-metal with a curved windscreen and manhole in the roof. It is heated via a radiator supplied with engine oil. Gear change is pressure assisted by means of a gearshift lever with pre-selector for ease of operation. The cargo body has steel sideboards and a floor made of waterproof plywood covered with an anti-slip layer. The core of the truck is the chassis, and this design concept facilitates a simple distribution of forces from a trailer and/or additional equipment (such as a snow plough blade) onto the structure.

SPECIFICATIONS

Type:	cargo truck
Manufacturer:	TATRA
Powerplant:	TATRA T3B-928.10
Horsepower:	308
Transmission:	10 + 2
Length:	7.96m (26.11ft)
Width:	2.6m (8.53ft)
Height:	2.99m (9.8ft)
Weight:	26,000kg (57,200lb)
Ground clearance:	0.36m (1.18ft)
Armament:	none
Crew:	1
Top speed:	120km/h (75mph)
Range:	900km (563 miles)
Fording:	1.2m (3.93ft)
Gradient:	60 percent
Configuration:	6 x 6

T815-260R24

This is a special 6 x 6 medium mobility chassis with front-wheel drive disconnect, equipped with a Multilift Mk IV load-handling unit and capable of transporting flatracks or heavy containers loaded up to the maximum payload weight of 15,000kg (33,000lb). Equipped with a special adaptor "H-frame", it can handle European standardized containers. Standard equipment on the vehicle includes all-wheel drive with front axle drive disconnect, ABS, and cross and inter-axle differential locks. TATRA trucks are grouped into so-called "families" for ease of manufacture and standardization of parts. The ARMAX family is composed of trucks or chassis based on production commercial vehicles, which meet European emission, noise and axle load standards. The FORCE family are special trucks or chassis, both commercial and military, which use several different makes of water-cooled engines, special or automatic transmissions, and other high-performance design features enhancing the offroad mobility of the chassis. There is no doubt that the company's vehicles are well designed and proven: over 355,000 trucks and chassis using TATRA concepts have been produced since World War II. The range has been especially successful in Eastern Europe and in the former Soviet Union.

SPECIFICATIONS

Type:	logistics truck
Manufacturer:	TATRA
Powerplant:	TATRA T3B-928.60
Horsepower:	340
Transmission:	10 + 2
Length:	8.35m (27.39ft)
Width:	2.5m (8.2ft)
Height:	3.14m (10.3ft)
Weight:	28,700kg (63,140lb)
Ground clearance:	0.31m (1.01ft)
Armament:	none
Crew:	1
Top speed:	95km/h (59.37mph)
Range:	600km (375 miles)
Fording:	1.2m (3.93ft)
Gradient:	69 percent
Configuration:	6 x 6

T815-260R81

This vehicle is a special 8 x 8 mobility chassis with front-wheel drive disconnect and equipped with a Multilift Mk IV load-handling unit. The engine is air-cooled and supercharged with eight cylinders. The clutch is a single disc with a Belleville washer, and the gearbox is 10-speed mechanical, synchromeshed with a pneumatic gearshift booster and an electro-pneumatic engagement of normal or reduced drive mode. Brake units are equipped with automatic play adjustment. The TATRA chassis design idea is based on the time-proved idea of a backbone tube. No other truck can follow an uneven road profile in the same way as a TATRA truck. Excellent driving characteristics, especially in offroad environments, result from the special design of the chassis, first of all that of the sturdy backbone tube, consisting of the central load-carrying tube, independently suspended half-axles and cross-members. In comparison with a conventional-designed truck, this means a very rigid load-carrying structure, distinguished mainly by several times higher torsion strength and very high bend strength. A low torsion and bending load transferred to a superstructure enables the manufacturer to join it with the undercarriage in a simple manner. In addition, add-on equipment attachments are of simple design.

SPECIFICATIONS

Type:	*logistics truck*
Manufacturer:	*TATRA*
Powerplant:	*TATRA T3B-928.60*
Horsepower:	*340*
Transmission:	*10 + 2*
Length:	*8.68m (28.47ft)*
Width:	*2.5m (8.2ft)*
Height:	*4m (13.12ft)*
Weight:	*32,000kg (70,400lb)*
Ground clearance:	*0.3m (0.98ft)*
Armament:	*none*
Crew:	*1*
Top speed:	*90km/h (56.25mph)*
Range:	*650km (406 miles)*
Fording:	*1.2m (3.93ft)*
Gradient:	*63 percent*
Configuration:	*8 x 8*

T816-6MWV27

This is a platform truck that has been specifically designed to operate in temperature extremes. The TATRA T816 range has a 6 x 6 configuration with permanent drive of both rear axles and an option to switch to front axle drive if need be. The front axle suspension consists of torsion bars, while the rear axles have air bellows and spring coils. Engine choice is as follows: Cummins M11 ISM 400 water-cooled in-line six-cylinder (for 6 x 6 vehicles), Deutz water-cooled, eight-cylinder 400 kW (for 8 x 8 vehicles), or MTU water-cooled, 12-cylinder 610 kW (for 8 x 8 vehicles). Gearbox configuration is as follows: automatic, 6 speed plus 1 reverse or 10 speed plus 1 reverse (for 8 x 8 vehicles). The electronically controlled transmission is incorporated directly into the backbone tube and forms an integral part of the chassis structure. This design makes it possible for the transmission to work also as a transfer box, thus no transfer box is needed. The transmission has a number of useful features, including a so-called "limp-home" function and a shift-and-fault indicator. The cab is the all-metal type, with two cabin doors, a manhole in the roof, two full-size seats and an emergency seat located on the engine cover. The cabin tilt can be operated either manually or hydraulically.

SPECIFICATIONS

Type:	*cargo truck*
Manufacturer:	*TATRA*
Powerplant:	*Cummins ISM 400*
Horsepower:	*400*
Transmission:	*6 + 1*
Length:	*9.06m (29.72ft)*
Width:	*2.55m (8.36ft)*
Height:	*3.55m (11.64ft)*
Weight:	*26,000kg (57,200lb)*
Ground clearance:	*0.36m (1.18ft)*
Armament:	*none*
Crew:	*1*
Top speed:	*104km/h (65mph)*
Range:	*600km (375 miles)*
Fording:	*1.2m (3.93ft)*
Gradient:	*60 percent*
Configuration:	*6 x 6*

T816-6VWN9T

This semi-trailer prime mover is designed to haul semi-trailers transporting tanks, armoured personnel carriers and other heavy vehicles up to a maximum weight of 74,000kg (162,800lb) both on roads and on rugged terrain. The prime mover is also designed to operate in temperature extremes, high air humidity and in dusty environments (air conditioning is an option for the cab but is not fitted as standard). The fully automatic electronically controlled 10-speed transmission has hydraulic power shift, integral torque biasing lockable inter-axle differential, limp-home function and fault indicator. The front and rear axles have independent suspension sprung by leaf springs and telescopic shock absorbers. The powerful engine is the MTU 12V 183 TD22, which is a water-cooled, four-stroke, turbocharged and charge-air-cooled direct injection diesel unit. The vehicle has left-hand power-assisted steering, and is fitted with two winches that have cables with operating lengths of 70m (230ft) each. An auxiliary winch has an operating length of 150m (492ft). The brake system comprises wedge-type self-adjusting brake units, while the emergency brake is a spring type that acts on the wheels of the rear axles.

SPECIFICATIONS

Type:	*prime mover*
Manufacturer:	*TATRA*
Powerplant:	*MTU 12V 183 TD22*
Horsepower:	*800*
Transmission:	*10 + 2*
Length:	*9.02m (29.59ft)*
Width:	*2.78m (9.02ft)*
Height:	*3.51m (11.51ft)*
Weight:	*43,800kg (96,360lb)*
Ground clearance:	*0.4m (1.31ft)*
Armament:	*none*
Crew:	*1*
Top speed:	*85km/h (53.12mph)*
Range:	*1000km (625 miles)*
Fording:	*1.25m (4.1ft)*
Gradient:	*32 percent*
Configuration:	*8 x 8*

T816 8 X 8

The T816 forms the backbone of a whole family of military vehicles produced by TATRA. The example shown above is the logistics truck. Other vehicles in the range include a fuel tanker, which has four independent drums and hoses that make it possible to refuel four vehicles at once via fast-clip high-pressure tails or fast-clip filling guns. The water tanker version has a stainless steel tank designed for the transport of drinking water for front-line troops with baffles and bulkheads inside. The engine common to all variants is a water-cooled, four-stroke tur-bocharged model with direct diesel injection. The transmission is electronically controlled, fully automatic and is integrated into the chassis backbone tube. The vehicle has a limp-home function and shift-and-fault indicator. A crane is mounted on the rear of the logistics truck, which has a maximum horizontal capacity of 1000kg (2200lb) and a maximum load capacity of 2945kg (6479lb). Manually tiltable, it has hydraulically extendable supporting legs. The cab is of all-metal construction with two doors, flat split roof and manhole in the roof. The cargo body has a steel frame, aluminium side boards and a floor made of water-resistant plywood with an anti-slip surface.

SPECIFICATIONS

Type:	logistics truck
Manufacturer:	TATRA
Powerplant:	Deutz BF8M 1015C diesel
Horsepower:	536
Transmission:	6 + 1
Length:	9.37m (30.74ft)
Width:	2.6m (8.53ft)
Height:	3.19m (10.46ft)
Weight:	30,800kg (67,760lb)
Ground clearance:	0.41m (1.34ft)
Armament:	none
Crew:	1
Top speed:	120km/h (75mph)
Range:	1000km (625 miles)
Fording:	1.25m (4.1ft)
Gradient:	37 percent
Configuration:	8 x 8

UNIMOG

The Unimog has a long history, being designed in 1946 and first produced in 1948. Though there are a number of variants in the range, all vehicles have the same basic layout with the engine and cab at the front and the cargo area at the rear. Most of the military variants have a two-door cab with a hard or soft top and a windscreen that folds down onto the bonnet. The cargo area has a drop tailgate, drop sides, removable bows and a tarpaulin cover. All Unimogs have excellent cross-country performance, being fitted with four-wheel drive and differential locks on both the front and rear axles. On roads it is usual for only the rear wheels to be engaged, while on rough terrain all wheels are engaged. In use with nearly 40 countries worldwide, Unimogs are used in a variety of roles, including ambulance, command vehicle, firefighting vehicle, radio vehicle, workshop and prime mover for artillery pieces up to 105mm in calibre. Options include a fully enclosed cab, generator, snow ploughs and winch. Mercedes-Benz are constantly updating the Unimog with different transmissions and powerplants. Essentially, however, the shell of the vehicle is much the same as it was when it rolled off the production line only three years after the end of World War II.

SPECIFICATIONS

Type:	light truck
Manufacturer:	Mercedes-Benz
Powerplant:	OM 352 diesel
Horsepower:	536
Transmission:	4 + 4
Length:	5.54m (18.17ft)
Width:	2.3m (7.54ft)
Height:	2.7m (8.85ft)
Weight:	5250kg (11,550lb)
Ground clearance:	0.44m (1.44ft)
Armament:	none
Crew:	1
Top speed:	82km/h (51.25mph)
Range:	700km (437 miles)
Fording:	1.2m (3.93ft)
Gradient:	70 percent
Configuration:	4 x 4

INDEX